LMSW Passing Score

LMSW Passing Score

Your Comprehensive Guide to the ASWB Social Work Licensing Exam

Jeremy Schwartz, LCSW

Seeley Street Press

Published in the United States of America by:
Seeley Street Press
Takoma Park, MD 20912

First Printing, 2022

Paperback ISBN: 979-8-9865570-2-1
Hardcover ISBN: 979-8-9865570-4-5
e-Book ISBN: 979-8-9865570-3-8

Publisher's Cataloging-in-Publication Data:
Names: Schwartz, Jeremy, author.
Title: LMSW passing score: Your comprehensive guide to the ASWB social work licensing exam / Jeremy Schwartz, LCSW
Description: 2023 Edition. | Takoma Park, MD : Seeley Street Press, [2022]
Identifiers: ISBN 979-8-9865570-4-5
Subjects: LCSH: Social workers – Certification – United States. | Social service – United States – Examinations – Study guides. | Social service – United States – Examinations, questions, etc.
Classification: LOC: HV40.52.A74 2022 | DDC: 361.3076—dc23

CONTENTS

CONTENTS

If you're like most readers picking up this book, chances are you already have significant knowledge and skills in social work. You've spent the past two to three years, at least, in an accredited Master of Social Work program. You may have an undergraduate degree in social work or a related field as well. Now, having reached the termination phase of your MSW studies, you are preparing to pursue licensure or certification in your U.S. state or Canadian province as a professional social worker.

All 50 U.S. states, as well as the District of Columbia, the U.S. Virgin Islands, Guam, the Northern Mariana Islands, and all 10 Canadian provinces are members of the Association of Social Work Boards (ASWB®), the organization that owns and maintains the social work licensing exams. Each state or province has its own licensing terms and requirements. When an exam is required, earning a passing score is a key milestone in your professional journey as a social worker.

The ASWB Master's Level exam is intended for social workers who have completed a Master of Social Work degree. The ASWB also administers the Associate, Bachelor's, Advanced Generalist, and Clinical Exams, which are used in some states and provinces for various levels of licensure.

Your passing score on this exam will get you to the next step as you embark on your social work career. Reach out to me at jeremy.d.schwartz@gmail.com if I can be of help in any way. I am available for private tutoring, and in any case would love to hear about your experiences working with this book.

Wishing you success on this journey,

Jeremy

A Brief Overview of this Guide

1. A social worker applies to his state board of social work to become a Licensed Master Social Worker and receives authorization to register for the ASWB Master's Level exam. The social worker is aware that he has significant test anxiety. In order to adequately prepare for the exam and address his test anxiety, the social worker should NEXT:

A. Buy lots of different study materials
B. Panic
C. Give up
D. Make a plan for success

The correct answer is D. **Make a plan for success**.

As you begin studying for your social work licensing or certification exam, it is important that you have a plan to adequately prepare so that you can walk into the testing center with confidence on your exam date. By purchasing this guide and beginning to read it, you have already taken an important first step in this process.

This comprehensive guide contains a large amount of content as well as practice material to support your success on the exam. Included in this book is information you should know about the exam, an introduction to the licensure or certification application process, guidance on how to prepare for the exam, a section for developing your personal study plan, and test-taking tips specific to the ASWB Master's Level social work licensing examination. Also included is extensive content review covering the material you need to know for the exam, a full-length practice exam, and detailed answer explanations for each question on the practice exam.

With such an extensive amount of material, you might at first be overwhelmed and not know where to start. Do not worry! The section on developing your personalized study plan will leave you with a clear roadmap to success on test day.

As you complete the personalized study plan, think realistically about the commitment you are making and your willingness to complete the work you assign yourself. Make sure to include a review of the Ten Test-Taking Tips section, as well as the Content Review sections.

The Content Review portion of this guide is composed of four chapters, each covering an area of social work that will hopefully feel familiar from the coursework you completed in your Master of Social Work graduate program. This section covers Human Development and Behavior; Assessment and Intervention Planning; Intervention Methods and Theories; and Professional Values, Ethics, and Relationships.

Following the content review portion of this guide, I have included a full-length, 170-question practice exam. These questions are entirely original and have never before been published. This practice exam will allow you to get a feel for the format of the test and to practice applying your test-taking techniques.

Along with the practice exam, I have included detailed answer explanations for each question. These explanations will give you the content needed to understand any questions that you answer incorrectly. They also provide information that may be helpful in further developing your understanding of questions that you do answer correctly but may not have been fully confident about.

Read on for some guidance on how to make the best use of this book.

How to Use this Guide

It is normal for social workers and social work students to feel overwhelmed when studying for the ASWB social work licensing exams. With so much content covering 2 years or more of graduate level education, not to mention content that may be outside of your areas of specialization, where do you even begin?

You have come to the right place. This book will give you the content review you need as well as a practice exam so you can get to know the question types and how to best apply your social work knowledge to earn your passing score.

You can certainly read this book cover to cover, and I hope that you will. That is the best way to get the information and test-taking practice that you need in your exam prep journey. I've organized this book so that you start with general information about the exam, then build your SMART study plan, review the 4 content areas covered on the exam, and end with a practice test so that you know what to expect when you get to the testing center.

If you do choose to skip around this book, make sure to start with the SMART study plan. I recommend actually taking the time to think through your study plan and follow the guidance in this section. When you set SMART goals, you are more likely to achieve them!

Once you have your study plan in place, you will be ready to get started on your path to success. Make sure to follow your plan, revising it if necessary, but without falling into procrastination. Use the Content Review sections to master the knowledge you need, and the practice test to work on your test-taking skills. You are ready for this!

What You Should Know About the LMSW Exam

The ASWB Master's Level examination is the test required to obtain your license or certification as a professional social worker. It is administered by the Association of Social Work Boards, a non-profit organization made up of the boards of social work in all 50 U.S. states, as well as the District of Columbia, the U.S. Virgin Islands, Guam, the Northern Mariana Islands, and all 10 Canadian provinces.

Depending on where you live or where you plan to practice social work, the credential you are seeking may be known as the LMSW, LGSW, APSW, CSW, or RSW. For any of these licenses, certifications, or registrations, the ASWB Master's Level examination is the test given once you have completed (or are about to complete) your Master of Social Work degree.

This exam does not require supervised experience, beyond your field learning internships, and so the knowledge you are tested on is based on standard MSW curriculum content. By this point, you likely have developed specialized knowledge in particular areas of social work practice, and you have also learned about policies and resources in particular cities or counties. However, because the test questions are the same for social workers in very different geographic areas and fields of practice, the exam requires that you show a basic level of knowledge about a very wide range of topics.

The exam is not a measure of how effective you are as a social worker. It is also not a measure of how intelligent you are. It is still important, though, in ensuring that clients receive the services of knowledgeable, qualified social workers.

For you, earning your license will allow you to have more of an impact, make a better living, and help more people. The majority of MSW graduates are in jobs that require licensure, and jobs requiring licensure pay, on average, nearly $3,000 more than jobs that do not require licensure.

Since this exam matters for your career, **preparation is key**. The exam covers 4 content areas, which are covered in the content review section of this guide:

Human Development and Behavior
Assessment and Intervention Planning
Intervention Methods and Theories
Professional Values, Ethics, and Relationships

Before 2023, ASWB exam questions all had 4 answer choices (A, B, C, and D). Starting in January 2023, some test questions will have 3 answer choices (A, B, and C) while other questions will have 4 answer choices (A, B, C, and D). The practice exam in this book is updated for this 2023 format.

So, if you hear rumors about how the exam is changing this year, this is it! There are no other significant changes that have been announced for this year, and nothing you need to do differently in order to prepare. Just know that some questions will only have 3 answer choices, so it won't cause any surprise or confusion on your exam day.

As always, it is important to answer every question and not leave any questions blank. While most multiple choice exams give you a 25% chance of guessing correctly even if you do not know the answer, this update to the exam gives you even more of a benefit for guessing. On questions with 3 answer choices, you have a 33% chance of guessing correctly even when you have no idea which answer is correct.

Of course, you should incorporate the other test-taking techniques in this guide as well, along with a thorough review of the content. Still, let this change be to your benefit as you work toward your passing score.

Which exam do I need to take to get licensed?

Each state or provincial board of social work sets its own standards for social work licensure at various levels. Since you've picked up this book, you are hopefully preparing to take the ASWB Master's Level social work licensing exam. This exam is typically required for social workers applying for licensure after they have completed a MSW degree but who have not yet accumulated clinical hours.

Unfortunately, many social workers struggle with passing this exam. According to the most recent data available, approximately 75% of test takers pass this exam on their first attempt. That leaves, unfortunately, one quarter of exam candidates who have to retake the exam, or who may give up on licensure altogether.

Still, three quarters of social workers have been able to pass this exam the first time, and I want to make sure that you can join them (and perhaps increase that number)!

Why do I have to take this exam?

To earn your license as a professional, Master's level social worker! Licensure is a form of consumer protection. I encourage social workers to develop a positive relationship with the reality of having to take this exam. By taking this exam, you are doing something positive for yourself, for the clients you will serve, and for the social work profession. Even if you have heard negative remarks from others about the exam, I encourage you to develop your own story through your own experience.

How can I pass the exam?

Succeeding on the ASWB Master's Level exam and earning your passing score takes more than knowing the content. You will also need to learn how the test questions are written and how to think through each type of test question.

You can indeed study for this exam, and you do need to study for this exam.

I especially recommend using written materials to prepare, since this is a written test that requires reading comprehension and focus in reading. You may supplement your reading with videos or podcasts, but don't let that take the place of reading. It is important that your studying prepares you for both the content as well as the way in which you will be tested.

To do this, it is important that you pace yourself as you review each content area.

Success on the exam also requires mastering test anxiety, as well as practicing self-care, so that you can demonstrate your knowledge and skills on test day.

How long does it take to study for the LMSW exam?

I recommend devoting at least one month, and preferably three months, to preparing for this exam. During this time, it is important to set up a regular study schedule so that you can work through the material at a comfortable pace. Use the SMART study plan in this book to make a plan for success.

How many questions are on the ASWB exam?

There are 170 questions on each of the ASWB exams. However, only 150 questions count toward your score. The other 20 questions are experimental items that are included for purposes of validation and norming of their difficulty level. The experimental questions do not look any different from the scored questions, and are randomly inserted throughout your exam. You will have no way of knowing which questions count and which do not.

What is the format of the questions?

The exam is entirely multiple choice, and each question has either 3 possible answer choices (A, B, and C), or 4 possible answer choices (A, B, C, and D). Note that this is a new change for 2023. Before 2023, every question had 4 possible answer choices (A, B, C, and D). Either way, each question has only one correct answer. There are 3 types of questions that you will see:

Recall Questions

Recall questions test your memory of factual information that you can recognize or remember from your social work coursework or your studying for the exam.

Application Questions

Application questions test your ability to apply factual information to a case scenario. You may be asked what a social worker should do in a particular situation.

Reasoning Questions

Reasoning questions involve case vignettes that may have both relevant and irrelevant information. In a reasoning question, you are required to think critically and analyze a situation using your social work knowledge and skills.

How long will I have to complete the exam?

You will have 4 hours to complete this exam. You are allowed to take breaks, such as to use the restroom. However, the clock does not stop during these breaks, so they do count as part of your time. Most social workers complete the exam in less than 4 hours, so you should have time to go back and check your work.

If you find on practice tests that 4 hours is not enough, or if you have taken the exam before and had difficulty completing it in 4 hours, this suggests that you may benefit from testing accommodations.

When should I take the exam?

Give yourself just enough time to prepare, but no more. The reason for this is that most of your test prep occurred during your Master of Social Work program. The closer to your graduation date that you can take the exam, the better, so that the material will be fresh in your mind. In other words, don't put this off with the expectation that it will get easier. I recommend giving yourself about a month to study, but not more.

Where do I take the exam?

When you register for the exam, you will select a Pearson VUE test center location. At the Pearson VUE test center, there will be other test-takers who are there for a variety of academic and professional exams. So, while you may run into a classmate or colleague there, you may also find architects, engineers, or nurses. Do not be surprised if other test takers are there for more or less time than you are, as they are likely taking very different types of exams.

The exam is administered by computer in a highly secure testing environment. Unless you are approved for a specific testing accommodation that includes access to food or water, you will not be able to bring in any food or drink. You will also have to leave any personal items in a locker for the duration of the exam. Expect to encounter airport-style security measures such as showing that your pockets are empty, as well as validating your fingerprint when you enter the testing room and whenever you return from a break.

Are testing accommodations available?

There are many challenges to passing the licensing exam, including difficulty completing all questions within the 4 hour timeframe as well as language barriers. If you have been diagnosed with a learning disability or a condition such as ADHD or anxiety, you may be able to request testing accommodations. This must be done *before* you register for your exam.

The purpose of testing accommodations is to allow social workers who have physical or mental health disabilities, learning disabilities, or limited English proficiency to successfully demonstrate their knowledge and skills on the exam.

ASWB calls these testing accommodations *non-standard testing arrangements*. People with disabilities are protected by law and all state or provincial boards of social work will allow accommodations for people with disabilities. Some social work boards will also allow accommodations for people with limited English proficiency.

A disability is defined as a physical or mental impairment that substantially limits one or more major life activities. A healthcare provider can provide documentation of your disability.

In addition to accommodations for disabilities and for limited English proficiency, the ASWB also allows accommodations for lactating individuals.

Some examples of testing accommodations include:

- Access to food or water
- Access to a private lactation space
- Additional time
- English dictionary
- Individual testing room
- Live test reader
- Physical access arrangements
- Printed exam

There is no additional fee for testing accommodations.

Is the exam different from state to state?

The exam is the same in every U.S. state, territory, and Canadian province that requires the ASWB Master's Level exam. You can even reside in one state, apply for a social work license in a different state, and sit for the exam in a third state. The only difference is that some states require you to complete your MSW degree before you register for the exam, while other states will allow you to sit for the exam during the final semester of your MSW program.

How many questions do I need to answer correctly in order to pass?

The number of questions that you need to answer correctly to pass the ASWB Master's Level exam will depend on the exact test that you take. Because the exams are normed for difficulty, you will have questions that are known to be, on average, "easier" (more candidates get them correct) or "harder" (fewer candidates get them correct). The number of questions required for a passing score can be anywhere from 93 to 107 out of the 150 scored questions.

Is the test the same every time?

Yes and no. Test questions are randomized such that each administration of the exam will include different questions presented in a different order. However, the exam will always follow the ASWB content outline and will cover material that is based on the ASWB's analysis of social work practice.

How do I contact my state's licensing board?

Using an internet search engine, you can enter terms such as "social work license" or "board of social work" along with the name of your state or province. Licensing boards are often housed within state agencies such as a Department of Education, Department of Health, or Department of Public Safety. You may also be provided with licensing application information from your graduate school of social work.

How do I sign up for the exam?

There are several steps that you must complete in order to schedule your exam. The first step is to apply for licensure with your state or provincial board of social work. Once your application has been processed, the state board will notify you that you are authorized to register for the exam. They will also provide your information to the ASWB so that you will be able to register.

Once you have received this authorization, visit the ASWB's exam registration website to register and pay the exam fee.

Once your registration has been processed, ASWB will send you an Authorization to Test email. Once you receive this email, you will be able to access the Pearson VUE scheduling site in order to choose the location, date, and time of your exam.

Testing appointments with Pearson VUE are based on availability, so it is normal to have to wait a few weeks or to have to travel some distance in order to take the exam.

Applying for Social Work Licensure

Each U.S. state, territory, and Canadian province has its own process for applying for licensure or certification. Look up your state licensing board or provincial college of social work to get started. You will need to submit an application form and payment, and will likely need to obtain or request your transcript from the college or university where you completed your MSW program. You may also need to submit proof that you have completed particular requirements, such as training about your obligations as a mandated reporter of suspected child abuse or neglect.

Because each state, territory, and province has its own requirements and processes, it is important to check with them directly. Requirements and processes for licensure or certification also may change from time to time. You can find your board's website and contact them directly with any questions.

Once you have applied for your social work license or certification, you will receive notification of your eligibility to sit for the ASWB exam.

Registering to Take the ASWB Exam

The first step in registering to take the ASWB Master's Level exam is to receive approval from your state or provincial board to register with ASWB for the exam. Once you receive this, you can begin the registration process with ASWB. This requires a separate form and payment submitted directly to ASWB.

Once this is complete, ASWB will send you an authorization to test notice by email. This notice will contain the instructions for registering with Pearson VUE, a private company that administers many different types of exams.

Pearson VUE maintains a network of test centers around the world, allowing you to take the exam in a location convenient to you. You can even take the exam in a different state than the state to which you have applied for licensure. At the test center, there will be other exam candidates taking different exams for any number of different academic or professional purposes. At times, there can be a wait for an appointment at a Pearson VUE test center, so try to register early and don't hesitate to look into available appointments at different test center locations.

Which ASWB exam do I need to take?

The ASWB develops and administers 4 different exams: the Bachelor's Level exam, the Master's Level exam, the Advanced Generalist exam, and the Clinical Level exam. There is also an Associate Level in some states, which uses the Bachelor's Level exam with a lower required score.

This book focuses on the Master's Level exam, which is the most widely utilized and most commonly taken. Depending on your state or province, this may be the exam needed in partial fulfillment of the requirements to become a Licensed Master Social Worker, Licensed Social Worker, Licensed Graduate Social Worker, Advance Practice Social Worker, or Registered Social Worker.

Before you begin your preparation, it is important to confirm that you are preparing for the correct exam! Licensure terms such as LICSW or LSW can have different meanings in different states and provinces, but the ASWB exams are the same throughout the United States and in the Canadian provinces that utilize these exams.

To make sure you are preparing for the correct exam, you should check with your state or provincial board to find out the ASWB exam level that is required for the particular license that you need.

While this book is intended for ASWB Master's Level exam candidates, much of the content here can also be helpful for other ASWB exam levels. If you plan to take the Clinical Level exam as well in a few years, do save this book as it will be helpful to review.

Six Study Strategies to Prepare for Your Exam

In most graduate social work programs, assessment happens through written papers and supervised field experience, rather than through testing. It may have been a long time since you have taken a test, and an even longer time since you have taken a multiple-choice, standardized exam. For many social workers, the experience of sitting in a formal testing center taking an exam by computer may be entirely new. Even so, many social workers have passed this exam and, with adequate preparation, you can too.

Preparation for this exam is key, so here are the six study strategies you will need:

1. Brush up on content.

Having to study for an exam may be something you wish you did not have to do, but one silver lining in this process is that it is an opportunity to learn new things and refresh your knowledge and skills just as you are beginning your career as a professional social worker. Perhaps your MSW program was clinically focused and you have some gaps in knowledge about research and community organizing. Or, maybe you learned mostly psychodynamic theories in graduate school and you could benefit from learning about cognitive and behavioral theories.

While test-taking skills will help you earn your passing score, there is no substitute for understanding the material. The exam requires more than memorization. It is important to truly comprehend the material so that you can actively and thoughtfully apply the material to micro, mezzo, and macro social work practice.

Use this book as your guide to the social work theories and applications that you will demonstrate your knowledge about on test day. The ASWB publishes content outlines describing exactly what information can be included on the exam. This book includes sections covering many of the topics listed on the ASWB content outline for this exam, so make sure to read every section and give special attention to any material that appears unfamiliar. As you develop a better understanding of the content, you will be better able to apply it in the different situations you are asked about in the test questions.

2. Build up your endurance.

I recommend setting aside 4 hour blocks of time for your studying. This is indeed a large amount of time – and, it will help you build up your ability to focus in preparation for the exam.

Of course, you can and should make good use of smaller windows of time as well, but those longer study sessions can give you the time you need to really master the content and work through practice questions, all while building up your ability to stay engaged and focused for the 4 hours that you will have at the testing center.

This does not mean that you need to work straight through the 4 hours with no breaks! I recommend taking short breaks when needed and then coming right back to the material, just as you will do during the exam.

3. Give yourself at least a few weeks, and ideally a few months, to prepare.

One of the biggest mistakes I have seen new social workers make with this exam is scheduling the test without giving themselves enough time to prepare.

With enough time and preparation, you can pass this exam. I recommend giving yourself at least 4 weeks, and up to 3 months (especially if you are working full-time), so that you can master the content and take as many practice tests as you need. Then, you can go into the testing center confident that you are ready to earn your passing score.

Once you have scheduled your test date, use the personal study plan worksheet in the next section to set up your plan for success.

4. Be selective about your study materials.

There are a number of books and other products on the market designed to help test-takers for the ASWB exams, and they vary widely in quality. Before purchasing a book or other product, make sure that it is actually written by a social worker with a graduate degree – not by anonymous writers at a test preparation company. If you find a book, online program, or mobile app with typos, content errors, or poorly written practice questions, move on so that you don't devote unnecessary time and energy to something that will not be helpful.

Since you already have this book, you will not need much else to study from. No one book can cover every piece of information, but there is still a great deal of information contained within these pages. If you wish to read more about an area of content, you can use the textbooks and articles from your graduate program.

For additional practice questions, I have published a 150-question exam with answer explanations, titled *Pass the LMSW Exam: A Practice Test for the ASWB Master's Level Social Work Licensing Examination* (2022, Seeley Street Press). You can purchase a copy anywhere books are sold. If your local library provides e-books through Overdrive, you can request this practice exam through that service as well.

5. Learn the perspective of "exam social work."

On the social work licensing exams, you are tasked with choosing the correct answers to how a social worker would handle a range of situations in an abstract, theoretical environment. Because the social worker we collectively imagine on the exam does not work at a particular agency, nor in a particular city or county, we cannot add any restrictions or limitations just because of specific policies in our agency settings or geographic areas.

Therefore, for purposes of the exam, you should select the answer choice that fits the "by the book" practice of social work independent of any particular constraints that are not described in the question.

6. Do not worry.

Because this is a high stakes exam, it is normal to experience test anxiety.

Be kind to yourself about this process, and do not add additional pressure by telling yourself that you have to pass the first time. While you can pass this exam on your first attempt, and in all likelihood you will, you do not have to. Once you pass your exam, it will not matter how many attempts you needed. Just as you show compassion toward your clients, make sure to show compassion toward yourself as well.

Nothing bad can happen from taking this exam, whether on the first attempt or on a subsequent attempt. While there is every reason to believe that you will achieve a passing score, especially as you are putting in the preparation by working through this book, there is no requirement that you pass on your first attempt. If you need to take the exam again, you will be required to wait 90 days, unless you qualify for an exemption. This will give you the time to further deepen your knowledge of the content as well as strengthen your test-taking skills. In some states, you can even obtain a limited permit to begin working as a social worker before getting that passing score. Again, there is nothing wrong with having to retake the exam.

Even so, you can pass this exam! So, go ahead and visualize yourself passing and visualize yourself becoming a licensed social worker.

Your SMART Study Plan

This section of the book is designed to help you develop your plan for success. It is important that you prepare for this exam so that you can go into the testing center with confidence. Of course, social workers are very busy people, and lack of time to study is one of the main barriers to passing this exam. Let's come up with a plan so that you can find the time you need to ensure success. Have a growth mindset, knowing that your efforts will produce results!

Since we can't add more hours to the day, we instead have to think through how to make good use of the time we do have.

The first step in developing your study plan is to have an actual or anticipated test date. This is an important component of your plan because it will allow you to pace yourself in your preparation. This can be an actual test date for which you have registered, or it can be a target test date if you have not yet been able to register.

Studying for this exam will have to fit into your life. This might mean studying on the weekends, or it might mean taking some days off from work. For example, if it is currently May and you anticipate taking the exam in August, you can plan out how you will study over the three months that you have until your exam. If you are working full time, you might devote three hours each Saturday and Sunday to test prep. Or, you might choose two weeknights each week, during which you will study for two hours each time. You might even consider taking a week off from work so you can devote the time and attention you need to test prep.

Whatever you do, do not put this off! Stay on track with an accountability partner. Being accountable to someone in your life can be especially helpful. This person does not need to be a social worker. A family member or friend who can be supportive and also hold you accountable will be so helpful as you prepare for the exam. Use that support to stay motivated. One tip: consider if you can explain a particular concept to a classmate or colleague. If you have trouble, stay on that topic until you feel you can confidently describe the relevant concepts.

And, finally, set **SMART** goals and connect your learning to your goals! Write down *why* you are doing this so that you can look back at your purpose whenever you need to. While you are not in control of the eventual outcome, you are very much in control of the steps you take to get there.

SMART Goals

Specific

Make your goals as narrow and detailed as possible so that you can plan to do exactly what you set out to do.

Measurable

Make sure your specific objectives can be quantified. For example, the statement "I will read for one hour and make 10 flashcards" contains 2 measurable objectives.

Achievable

Set objectives that are attainable and realistic, and that fit into your life in a way that is sustainable. It is important that you continue to practice self-care and not become overly fatigued.

Relevant

Make sure that your study activities are indeed supportive of your goal. Key to relevancy is knowing what will be on the test! Of course, I don't mean the specific questions, which you can't know. Instead, I'm referring to what the ASWB calls KSAs: knowledge, skills, and abilities. The ASWB has published a content outline that specifies exactly what the exam is meant to cover. Many of the topics from the content outline are covered in this book. Make sure you learn the content so you know the material that you are being tested on.

Time-Bound

A sense of urgency can be helpful in keeping you on track. Set a target date when you plan to take the exam, and then establish objectives along the way that prepare you to pass on test day. Make good use of time, but avoid multitasking. Do not forget to take breaks! Prioritize self-care because *you need to fill your tank* to keep on track.

On the pages that follow, I offer a suggested study plan for when you have 4 weeks leading up to your test date, as well as a suggested study plan for when you have 12 weeks leading up to your test date. Choose the plan that is right for you, and check off the activities as you do them.

Ultimately, preparing for this exam requires readiness. There is no better time than this moment to get started. Go for it!

LMSW Four-Week SMART Study Plan

Four weeks may not seem like a lot of time, but there is so much you can do between now and test day! Here's my suggested study plan when you have one month between now and your exam. Check off each task as you complete it, and you should be in great shape for test day.

Today's date: _____

Test date (or approximate test date): _____

Week 1

Read the Content Review chapters on *Human Development and Behavior* and *Assessment and Intervention Planning*. Order a copy of **Pass the LMSW Exam: A Practice Test for the ASWB Master's Level Social Work Licensing Examination** (Seeley Street Press, 2022), or check it out from your library in either the print or digital format. Also, purchase a pack of index cards (at least 100 cards, 3" x 5" or larger, ideally in a variety of colors) to use next week.

Place a checkmark below when you have completed each task.

Read *Human Development and Behavior* chapter _____

Read *Assessment and Intervention Planning* chapter _____

Ordered *Pass the LMSW Exam* (Seeley Street Press, 2022) _____

Purchased index cards _____

Week 2

Read the Content Review chapters on *Intervention Methods and Theories* and *Professional Values, Ethics, and Relationships.* Review the chapters you read last week and make flashcards for each term or concept in bold, except for those that you already know well. Take the practice test in *Pass the LMSW Exam* in one 4 hour sitting.

Place a checkmark below when you have completed each task.

Read *Intervention Methods and Theories* chapter _____

Read *Professional Values, Ethics, and Relationships* chapter _____

Created flashcards for *Human Development and Behavior* _____

Created flashcards for *Assessment and Intervention Planning* _____

Took practice test from *Pass the LMSW Exam* book _____

Week 3

Review the answer explanations from last week's practice test for any questions you answered incorrectly. Create flashcards for *Intervention Methods and Theories* and *Professional Values, Ethics, and Relationships.* Then, on two different days, for 1-2 hours each day, test yourself using your complete set of flashcards.

Place a checkmark below when you have completed each task.

Reviewed answer explanations in *Pass the LMSW Exam* book _____

Created flashcards for *Intervention Methods and Theories* _____

Created flashcards for *Professional Values, Ethics, and Relationships* _____

Tested self using flashcards for 1-2 hours _____

Tested self again using flashcards for 1-2 hours _____

Week 4

Take the practice test at the end of this book in one 4 hour sitting (with breaks), and check your answers when you have finished. Then take a day off from studying. On two different days, review the answer explanations for the questions you answered incorrectly.

Place a checkmark below when you have completed each task.

Took the practice test in one 4 hour sitting, with breaks _____

Took a day off from studying _____

Reviewed answer explanations (first half) _____

Reviewed answer explanations (second half) _____

Congratulations! You have completed the 4 week SMART study plan. You have put in the work, and you are ready for this. Best of luck!

If you have 12 weeks between now and your exam date, there is plenty of time to study well and still build in time for rest and self-care. Start your preparation today, and you will be able to go into the exam comfortable and confident. Check off each task as you complete it so you can track your progress.

Today's date: _____

Test date (or approximate test date): _____

Week 1

Read through the Six Study Strategies and Ten Test-Taking Tips sections in this book. Read the Content Review chapter on *Human Development and Behavior*. Order a copy of **Pass the LMSW Exam: A Practice Test for the ASWB Master's Level Social Work Licensing Examination** (Seeley Street Press, 2022) to use next week. Also, purchase a pack of index cards (at least 100 cards, 3" x 5" or larger, ideally in a variety of colors).

Place a checkmark below when you have completed each task.

Read Six Study Strategies and Ten Test-Taking Tips sections _____

Read *Human Development and Behavior* chapter _____

Ordered *Pass the LMSW Exam* (Seeley Street Press, 2022) _____

Purchased index cards _____

Week 2

Review the *Human Development and Behavior* chapter you read last week and make flashcards for each term or concept in bold, except for those that you already know well. Then, on a different day, test yourself using your flashcards for 1-2 hours.

Place a checkmark below when you have completed each task.

Created flashcards for *Human Development and Behavior* _____

Test self using flashcards for 1-2 hours _____

Week 3

This week, you will take your first full-length practice test. Set aside a 4 hour block of time when you won't be interrupted or distracted. Take the practice test in *Pass the LMSW Exam* in one 4 hour sitting.

Place a checkmark below when you have completed this task.

Took practice test from *Pass the LMSW Exam* book _____

Week 4

Review the answer explanations from last week's practice test for any questions you answered incorrectly. Then, on a different day, read the *Assessment and Intervention Planning* chapter and create flashcards for each term or concept in bold, except for those that you already know well.

Place a checkmark below when you have completed each task.

Reviewed answer explanations in *Pass the LMSW Exam* book _____

Read *Assessment and Intervention Planning* chapter _____

Created flashcards for *Assessment and Intervention Planning* _____

Week 5

Test yourself on your knowledge of the *Human Development and Behavior* material using your flashcards for 1 to 2 hours. Then, on a different day, test yourself on your knowledge of the *Assessment and Intervention Planning* material for 1 to 2 hours as well.

Place a checkmark below when you have completed each task.

Tested self using flashcards for 1-2 hours _____

Tested self again using flashcards for 1-2 hours _____

Week 6

Read the Content Review chapter on *Intervention Methods and Theories*. Create flashcards for each term or concept in bold, except for those that you already know well. On a different day, test yourself using your complete set of flashcards for 1-2 hours.

Place a checkmark below when you have completed each task.

Read *Intervention Methods and Theories* chapter _____

Created flashcards for *Intervention Methods and Theories* _____

Test self using flashcards for 1-2 hours _____

Week 7

Read the *Professional Values, Ethics, and Relationships* chapter in the Content Review section of this book. Create flashcards for each key term in **bold**.

Place a checkmark below when you have completed each task.

Read *Professional Values, Ethics, and Relationships* chapter _____

Created flashcards for *Professional Values, Ethics, and Relationships* _____

Week 8

Read the *NASW Code of Ethics* in its entirety. Write down 3 ethical principles from the *Code of Ethics* that surprised you, 2 ethical principles that you personally disagree with, and 1 ethical principle that you have seen a colleague fail to implement.

Place a checkmark below when you have completed each task.

Read *NASW Code of Ethics* _____

Wrote 3 ethical principles that were surprising, 2 that you disagree with, and 1 that you have seen a colleague fail to implement _____

Week 9

On two different days, test yourself using your flashcards based on the *Professional Values, Ethics, and Relationships* chapter.

Place a checkmark below when you have completed each task.

Tested self on *Professional Values, Ethics, and Relationships* flashcards (first day) _____

Tested self on *Professional Values, Ethics, and Relationships* flashcards (second day) _____

Week 10

Take the practice test at the end of this book in one 4-hour sitting – with breaks, of course! Then, take at least 2 days off from studying. Check in on your self-care routine and make sure you are practicing self-care.

Place a checkmark below when you have completed each task.

Took practice test from this book in one 4-hour sitting _____

Took at least 2 days off from studying _____

Practiced self-care _____

Week 11

Review the answer explanations for each question on the practice test from this book that you answered incorrectly.

Place a checkmark below when you have completed each task.

Reviewed answer explanations for test in this book _____

Week 12

Prioritize self care in an active way. Briefly study any content areas in which you feel you need additional review, but do not stress yourself out.

Place a checkmark below when you have completed each task.

Prioritized self care _____

Briefly studied content where needed _____

Stopped self from stressing out _____

Congratulations! You have completed the 12 week SMART study plan. You have put in the work, and you are ready for this. Best of luck!

Ten Test-Taking Tips for the LMSW Exam

1. Take your time.

The ASWB allows four hours to complete the exam, which is typically more than enough time to read every question thoroughly and to think through the answer choices. If you find on practice exams that you do not have enough time, it is worth it to pursue the process of requesting testing accommodations. In any case, this is not the type of exam on which you should need to rush. You may see an answer that looks correct, but it may not be the best answer. Reading the questions and each answer choice carefully can make the difference between passing and not passing, so take your time and choose the *best* answer from the choices given.

2. Pay attention to qualifying words.

Words such as FIRST, NEXT, BEST, MOST, NOT, and EXCEPT play a critical role in the meaning of the test questions. When you see one of these words, pay close attention, as there may be more than one answer choice that looks correct and seems to represent good social work practice.

For "FIRST" questions, your task is to identify the correct action a social worker should take at that exact moment in the helping process. If math is your thing, consider this as an "order of operations" word problem! During the engagement phase, for example, the correct action is often related to reciprocal communication and validation. During the assessment phase, on the other hand, a correct action may be related to exploration or obtaining collateral information.

Similarly, for "NEXT" questions, your task is to identify the phase of the helping process at the point in time of the case vignette and to select the correct action for that point in time. For example, during the treatment planning phase, a necessary action may involve collaborating with a client to identify goals and objectives. Other answer choices may point to correct actions for other phases of the helping process.

"BEST" and "MOST" questions sometimes will involve multiple answer choices that appear correct. Make sure you have read every answer choice before selecting your answer. Even if an answer choice appears correct or fits with your experience in the field, it may not be the answer choice that most closely fits the particular case vignette or question.

3. Prioritize using Maslow's hierarchy of needs.

This exam requires paying close attention to the client's most immediate needs and meeting the client where they are to address what is most important at the moment of the social worker's intervention. For example, if a client needs food and shelter, the social worker's focus should be on helping the client to meet those basic needs rather than on the client's relationships and self-esteem.

This starts with knowing who your client is! When presented with a clinical case vignette, multiple individuals, such as the client's spouse or other family members, may be mentioned. Your client may be an individual, couple, family, group, organization, community, or the larger society. Make sure to notice who is the client or client system that is the focus of the social worker's engagement, assessment, treatment planning, or intervention.

4. Base your answers on content.

The ASWB exams test specific knowledge, skills, and abilities that social workers need in order to be effective in their work. Every question is testing your specific knowledge, skills, and/or your ability to apply your knowledge and skills when working with clients and client systems. For purposes of the exam, your knowledge, skills, and abilities should be drawn from your course readings and from this study guide, rather than from practice wisdom or knowledge gained in specific practice settings.

5. Accept the limitations of the question or case vignette.

When reading case vignettes, it can be tempting to imagine specific clients or practice settings from your field placement or employment experience. When this happens, you might accidentally add information to the case that is not written in the question stem. Make sure to answer the question based only on the information included. Often, the case vignettes place you as the social worker in an initial session with a client, in which you do not yet have much information about their presenting problem or history. Do not add or assume any information that is not presented.

6. Answer the specific question.

Before choosing an answer, make sure you understand exactly what the question is asking. Some of the answer choices might reflect familiar terms or "good social work," even if they do not answer the question. It is important to select the answer choice that directly answers the question as it is written. Answers that do not fit with the question stem, or that are too extreme for the case scenario, are not correct.

7. Use the stages of the helping process.

The mnemonic **Early Arrival PIE T**asting can help you remember the social work helping process, also known as the problem-solving process: **engagement**, **assessment**, **planning**, **intervention**, **evaluation**, and **termination**. When thinking about how to answer what you as the social worker should do "FIRST" or "NEXT," take a step back and consider where you are at that moment in the problem-solving process. Take your work with the client one step at a time, and answer the question based on that one step. In the first session, your focus should be on engagement. Respond to clients with validation, acknowledging their feelings and "meeting the client where they are." Your focus in the engagement phase is to build rapport, not to diagnose or intervene. Often, with a case vignette question, that is as far as you need to go.

8. Notice the client's age.

If a case vignette tells you the age of a client or client's family member, this is likely to be relevant in selecting the correct answer. Stage theories such as Freud's stages of psychosexual development, Erikson's stages of psychosocial development, and Piaget's stages of cognitive development all involve typical ages during which an individual experiences a particular stage.

9. Use process of elimination.

As you read each answer choice, eliminate answers that are irrelevant to the question stem as well as those that are too extreme. Answers that use words such as "all," "always," and "never" are unlikely to be correct.

10. Prioritize the client and respect self-determination.

According to the *NASW Code of Ethics*, social workers' primary responsibility is to their clients. When there is a conflict between agency policies or practices and the client's needs, the social work role requires advocating for clients. Similarly, your assessment and treatment planning, for purposes of the exam, should be based on the client's needs and not based on your experience of what services are likely to be available based on proximity, cost, or insurance coverage. In the context of the exam, you should advocate for the client even if your experience leads you to believe this may not be effective.

One important concept that is often tested on the ASWB exams is the social work value of respecting client self-determination. You should not select an answer choice that involves the social worker imposing a viewpoint that is different than the client's stated wishes, except of course in cases of a client's imminent risk to self or others. Making a decision that goes against the client's self-determination should be reserved for serious threats to a person's safety.

The Social Work Helping Process

The social work helping process, also known as the problem-solving process, is your key to correctly answering many of the questions on this exam. In any case vignette, see if you can identify which stage of the helping process you have been placed in. Make sure to not get too far ahead of yourself! Remember that engagement and assessment come before planning, planning comes before intervention, and so on.

Engagement

Assessment

Planning

Intervention

Evaluation

Termination

Here's a mnemonic to help you remember the order of the stages:

Early Arrival PIE Tasting

A Special Note on Test Anxiety

Have you ever sat down for an exam and then, all of a sudden, your mind went blank? Having test anxiety is understandable. Test anxiety shows up when the test matters to you and when you care about how you do on the test. Each social worker is affected differently by having to take this exam, but test anxiety is extremely common.

It makes sense to be anxious. This is a difficult, high-stakes exam. Yet, while the test is important, it does not determine everything about your life. It does not even determine the future of your career. While you are putting in the work to pass, it is not essential that you pass on the first attempt. You will be able to take the test again if you need to.

Remember that *you have done this before*. It may have been a while, but you have done well on other exams and you have earned a Master's degree. You have already demonstrated that you are qualified and capable.

Ultimately, *a test is just a test*, and *how you do on a test only tells you how you do on a test* – nothing more.

Still, you may be feeling anxious. If you have test anxiety, what can you do about it?

Practice self-care.

When your mind and body are healthy, you can perform at your best. As you work through your study plan, make sure not to overdo it and become fatigued. It is important to take breaks during your study sessions as well as during the exam itself. Also, reward yourself for the good work you are doing. Build in some positive reinforcement as you take action on your study plan.

Use mindfulness exercises.

You may already have experience with mindfulness and meditation. If that is the case, use what you know, and make mindfulness a consistent part of your routine. Or, use an app such as Headspace or Calm to develop your mindfulness practice.

Start improving your sleep now.

Sleep is important for learning and memory. Give yourself time each evening to wind down and relax, and give yourself enough time to sleep each night.

Put the test in perspective.

Even though this is a high-stakes exam in general, the individual test date is *not* high-stakes. One quarter of social workers have to retake the exam, and that is entirely okay. You do not have to pass on the first attempt.

Manage your anxiety, but do not fight it.

Some level of anxiety can actually be helpful! Be kind to yourself when you notice that you are feeling anxious, and normalize the experience.

Content Review Section

The ASWB Master's Level exam requires you to know about many different social work topics, even if you plan to specialize in a specific field of practice. As you engage in content review, think about developing an understanding that is very broad, even if not so deep in every area. For this exam, you do not need to be an expert in everything! However, having a general knowledge about many topic areas is key.

The Content Review section of this book is divided into four chapters, each corresponding to one of the content areas covered on the exam:

Human Development and Behavior

Assessment and Intervention Planning

Intervention Methods and Theories

Professional Values, Ethics, and Relationships

Human Development and Behavior

Thinking Developmentally as a Social Worker

An understanding of human development and behavior throughout the lifespan is central to social work practice. **Development** can be defined as a series of age-related changes that an individual experiences over the lifespan. To understand human development, we use various theories, including developmental and ecological theories.

Theories tell us why we do what we do. It is important to understand theories of human development and behavior, as these theories inform every phase of the social work helping process. We have to understand how people function in order to effectively help people. Through the use of theory, we can engage in evidence-informed practice.

There are many potential pathways for successful development as a human. People are highly resilient and are often able to survive and thrive even in difficult circumstances. Still, throughout the life course, life events and transitions can pose challenges and create stress, even when these events and transitions are at times entirely welcome.

Human Growth and Development

Human development begins in utero and continues through to the end of life. There are a number of theories of human growth and development, which are often broken down into stages. While some stage theories only cover childhood, others are relevant to all periods of the lifespan from infancy to older adulthood. In addition to knowledge of specific stage theories, it is also helpful to know general aspects of normal development at each stage of the life course.

While much of human growth happens through gradual changes, there are also specific critical periods. **Critical periods** are early stages at which particular milestones are necessary for normal and healthy development. During **infancy**, significant physical, psychological, and emotional development occurs, including the infant's attachment bond with caregivers. A **secure attachment** bond makes the child feel safe to explore their environment.

In **early childhood**, children demonstrate rapid development in cognitive, language, motor, and social skills. School-age children develop through individual, family, and social processes and interactions as they continue through increasingly complex developmental stages. During the adolescent years, teenagers develop secondary sex characteristics, as well as changes in hormone levels. As adolescents mature they progress through new stages in moral development as well as sexual identity development. Depression, substance use, and eating disorders may be of particular concern during the adolescent years.

Early adulthood is also known as **emerging adulthood**. This is a period of transition into adult life roles, which traditionally have involved financial independence and even purchasing a home. In recent years, many young adults have been unable to achieve such stability, or have pursued non-traditional paths, as a result of changing economic and social trends.

Middle adulthood is characterized by Erikson's stage of generativity vs. stagnation. For many adults, generativity takes the form of parenting. Careers are often important during this time as well. Physical and cognitive changes in middle adulthood may create strengths and may also pose challenges. In middle adulthood, there is the potential for improved cognitive functioning as a result of neuroplasticity and increased learning. Individuals in middle adulthood are better able to manage emotions and navigate social situations than young adults are. There are physical changes during this time, as biological males experience a decline in testosterone levels, and biological females experience menopause. Medical problems may also emerge during this time.

In **older adulthood**, individuals experience a number of changes as they age. From a biological perspective, physical changes are linked to changes in the cells of the body, often associated with degenerative processes. As these changes occur, the body seeks to maintain homeostasis. Aging is discussed in more detail in the following section.

Aging

Successful aging is the maintenance of a person's adaptation and resilience for as long of a period as possible before the end of life. In using a biopsychosocial model, it is important to consider not only each aspect of aging individually, but also the interactions among biological, psychological, and social factors in a person's experience.

One common physical change with aging is age-related hearing loss, in which the person has an impaired ability to hear high-frequency sounds. This change is associated with slower gait, cognitive impairment, and increased mortality. Another physical change associated with aging is vision loss, which often takes the form of farsightedness. Age-related vision loss is associated with depression, cognitive decline, and increased mortality.

A person's sense of taste and smell also decline with age, with the sense of smell often reduced by nearly 50% once a person is 80 years old. Further, changes in the nervous system decrease the perception of pain, temperature, and other aspects of tactile sensation, increasing the risk of injury.

While such changes are common, they are not always predictable, and should not be seen as inevitable. Yet, by accounting for these changes when they occur, and with help, individuals can adapt to them and reduce risk of negative outcomes. Glasses, hearing aids, and other tools for adaptation can make a significant difference in a person's functioning.

Psychological factors associated with aging include the potential for increased stress. While stress is a normal part of life, older adults may encounter multiple major life events occurring at the same time. They may experience the death of loved ones, a loss of physical functioning, and decreased access to economic resources. Sometimes people cope with stress in healthy ways, but often people's ways of coping with stress can lead to negative consequences. In some older adults, anxiety and depression may be present. Anxiety and depression may also be associated with the person's experience of physical pain. Older adults may face challenges such as depression, dementia, and delirium. While **dementia** develops gradually, **delirium** has a more sudden onset.

Social factors also have a significant impact on a person's life as they age. **Ageism** and associated age discrimination, in particular, can be detrimental to a person's quality of life. While ageism and age discrimination can and do impact older adults at the micro level, ageism and age discrimination are also embedded in social institutions at a structural level, negatively impacting all older adults. From an intersectionality perspective, particular attention should be paid to the impacts of racism on older adults of color as well as the impacts of homophobia and transphobia on LGBTQ older adults. Socioeconomic status is a significant factor to consider as well. Many older adults live on a very low income, and at times may need to postpone retirement due to economic needs. Social isolation and experiences of loneliness, as well, significantly increase a person's risk for chronic disease.

Older adults are quite varied in all aspects of who they are. While some older adults require a great deal of assistance and support, others are in excellent health and live independently.

As mentioned earlier, it is important to use a biopsychosocial perspective in understanding a person's experience or difficulties as they age. For example, an older adult with physical health problems may be prescribed medication that they cannot afford due to the high cost of prescription drugs in their social environment (such as in the United States), and this social factor may lead to worsened physical and mental health outcomes.

Social workers play an important role in supporting successful aging by building on elders' strengths, supporting multigenerational families, providing mental health care, and advocating for policy changes.

Impact of Aging Parents on Adult Children

As their parents age, adult children often find themselves in the role of caregivers. Caregiving includes assistance with medical care arrangements, medical tasks (administering medication, checking blood pressure, etc.), household chores, and personal care. The caregiving role is often experienced as **role reversal**, as the adult children are filling needs for their parents that traditionally would be associated with parental caregiving for children. While caregiving has its benefits, it can also be burdensome for adult children who find themselves with limited time to juggle their many responsibilities.

Caregivers often experience difficulty with **caregiver stress,** which results from the physical and emotional strain of caring for another person. When family members provide care to older adults or disabled family members, they face stressors that can negatively affect their physical, emotional, and mental health. For example, caregivers are at an increased risk of depression. However, long-term caregiving can have positive outcomes in addition to these potential negative ones. Research has found that positive feelings and rewarding experiences of caregiving can mediate its negative effects.

Often, adult children who are caregivers to their parents also have children of their own. This is referred to as being in the **sandwich generation**, as they are "sandwiched" between two generations that both require their time and attention. While taking care of their aging parents, caregivers may worry about the impact of their caregiving on their own children as well.

Erikson's Stages of Psychosocial Development

According to psychosocial theory, human development involves the formation of identity, thoughts, emotions, and personality through interactions between the person and the society in which they live.

Erikson describes each life stage as being characterized by particular challenges that impact an individual's behavior and goals. The extent to which the person successfully masters the challenges of each stage impacts how they will cope with subsequent stages.

According to Erikson, there are 8 stages of psychosocial development. During each stage, the individual has a task, or "psychosocial crisis," that they must work through in order to master that stage and progress to the next one. Next to each psychosocial crisis listed here, in parentheses, are the typical ages at which individuals experience each stage. These age ranges are not included in Erikson's original text, and so you may see some small variations in the ages for each stage that listed in different books and articles.

Trust vs. Mistrust (Birth to 18 months of age)

During this stage of infancy, the infant faces the task of developing a sense of trust in themself and in their environment. Through the caregiver's meeting of the infant's needs, the infant develops a sense of inner goodness. If caregiving is not reliable, the infant may instead develop a sense of mistrust. Successful resolution of this stage is associated with the virtue of hope.

Autonomy vs. Shame and Doubt (18 months to 3 years of age)

During the toddler years, the child begins to hold on to and let go of objects. In doing this, the child is tasked with developing a sense of autonomous will. If they are given opportunities to do so, they can master this stage and believe in their own autonomy. If, instead, the child learns to expect that others who are bigger and stronger will defeat them, they will then develop feelings of shame and doubt. Successful resolution of this stage is associated with the virtue of purpose.

Initiative vs. Guilt (3 to 5 years of age)

During these early childhood years, considered the age of play, the child is able to move around, communicate, and pursue their curiosities. When their initiative is supported by the environment, the child is able to successfully master this stage. However, if the child's newly established conscience in the presence of overly critical adults or peers leads to a belief that the child is bad, the child will instead develop a pervasive sense of guilt.

Industry vs. Inferiority (5 to 12 years of age)

The child is now school aged, and is tasked with learning how to act and create in their environment. Mastery of this stage creates the capacity to see oneself as productive and able to contribute to those around them. However, if the child is not adequately recognized for their efforts, they may instead develop a sense of inadequacy and inferiority. Successful resolution of this stage is associated with the virtue of confidence.

Identity vs. Role Confusion (12 to 18 years of age)

The child now reaches adolescence and begins puberty. The adolescent's task is to integrate their childhood identities with their newfound biological and social reality. Mastery of this stage results in a consistent self-image around which the adolescent will begin to organize their life. Identity includes the experiences, beliefs, and values that make up the individual's sense of self. However, failure to resolve this stage with a stable sense of identity can instead lead to being unsure of who one is and where one fits in, along with feelings of disappointment and confusion. Successful resolution of this stage is associated with the virtue of fidelity.

Intimacy vs. Isolation (18 to 40 years of age)

Having reached adulthood and developed a secure sense of identity, the individual is now tasked with establishing intimacy on their own and with others. This includes friendships as well as satisfying sexual relationships. If the individual does not manage to enter into an intimate relationship, according to Erikson, they may instead develop a sense of isolation. Successful resolution of this stage is associated with the virtue of love.

Generativity vs. Stagnation (40 to 65 years of age)

In middle adulthood, the individual is tasked with establishing and guiding the next generation. Generativity may include raising children, as well as other ways of creating in the world. If the adult does not master this stage, they may instead develop a sense of stagnation. Successful resolution of this stage is associated with the virtue of care.

Integrity vs. Despair (65 years of age and older)

In older adulthood, the individual is tasked with looking back on and reviewing their life. If they feel that they have lived a good life and given back to others, they develop a sense of ego integrity. However, if the individual struggles to find meaning in what their life has been, they may instead experience disgust and despair. Successful resolution of this stage is associated with the virtue of wisdom.

Attachment and Bonding

A significant aspect of emotional development is **attachment.** Attachment theory is associated with the work of John Bowlby as well as the work of Mary Ainsworth. Attachment refers to lasting psychological connectedness between people. From an evolutionary perspective, attachment occurs in the context of a caregiver protecting a vulnerable child. According to the work of Bowlby, infants have an innate drive to form a primary attachment with one caregiver, who functions as the infant's secure base from which they explore the outside world.

There are four major attachment styles, although some are referred to using a few different terms:

Secure attachment refers to the healthiest attachment style, in which the child finds comfort in the presence of the caregiver. It involves a strong bond between the child and caregiver. Securely attached children will prefer the caregiver over strangers, find comfort in the caregiver, and comfortably explore their environment when the caregiver is around. Securely attached children show signs of distress when the caregiver leaves, but are quickly comforted by the caregiver's return. Children with secure attachment feel protected by their caregiver and trust that the caregiver will return.

Anxious, or **preoccupied attachment** refers to an ambivalent style, in which the child clings to the caregiver yet remains distressed. Though the caregiver may attempt to soothe the child, the child does not trust the caregiver's support.

Dismissive, or **anxious/avoidant attachment** is a pattern in which a child avoids the caregiver and does not seek comfort from them, even in times of distress. The child does not count on the caregiver to comfort them, as they may not find the caregiver to be attuned to their needs.

Fearful-avoidant, **disorganized**, or **chaotic attachment** is seen as an inconsistent connection between a child and caregiver, in which the child fears the caregiver. While the caregiver might sometimes provide support, which the child relies on, the caregiver is also at times unavailable or abusive.

Cognitive Development Theories

The brain is highly plastic, which allows for cognitive development throughout the lifespan. The most prevalent theories of cognitive development, however, focus on those aspects of development that happen during childhood.

Piaget's Theory of Cognitive Development

According to Piaget, the **sensorimotor** stage takes place from birth through the age of 2 years. During the sensorimotor stage, the infant engages in imitative play and begins to act intentionally. The infant develops a primitive form of logic in manipulating objects, and can retain images of objects it encounters. The infant develops a sense of meaning of particular signals, such as the idea that a babysitter's arrival signals the impending departure of the parent or caregiver. The infant also begins to develop some understanding of language and other symbols. Around 9 months of age, the infant develops **object permanence**, the understanding that objects still exist even when they cannot be seen.

The next stage in Piaget's theory of cognitive development is the **pre-operational stage**, which occurs from ages 2 through 7. ("Operational" in this context refers to mental operations.) During this stage, further development of symbolic meaning occurs. Included in symbolic meaning is the idea that words represent objects. Thus, the child develops language abilities, and can comprehend ideas about the past, present, and future. Children will engage in pretend and imaginative play. **Animism** is associated with the pre-operational stage, as well, and refers to the ascribing of life characteristics to inanimate objects. For example, the child may believe that a stuffed teddy bear has feelings. Thinking during this stage is concrete and egocentric, as the child does not yet understand that others may have different points of view than they do. **Egocentrism**, in Piaget's theory, refers to a young child's inability to see things from another person's point of view, and the inability to understand that another person's perspective may be different from one's own.

The child then progresses to the **concrete operational stage**, which occurs from the ages of 7 to 11 years of age. During this stage, the child begins to develop abstract thought and rules of logic. The child can play games that involve rules, and can understand logical implications as well as cause-and-effect relationships.

During the concrete operational stage, children learn the concept of **conservation**. A common "conservation task" is to pour water from a short, wide glass into a tall, narrow glass and ask the child which glass contains more water. With the theory of conservation, the child will understand that both contain the same amount of water even though the tall, narrow glass may look like it contains more. Memory trick: children develop a theory of *con*servation during the *con*crete operational stage.

The final stage in Piaget's theory of cognitive development is the **formal operational stage**, which begins at age 12 and continues throughout the lifespan. During this stage, individuals develop the ability to think abstractly and to solve problems using deductive reasoning, developing hypotheses and testing them. This stage allows for systematic and methodical problem solving.

A mnemonic for remembering Piaget's stages of cognitive development is the phrase *some people can fly*: sensorimotor, pre-operational, concrete operational, and formal operational.

Piaget also developed the concept of schemas, in which individuals assimilate and accommodate new information. **Assimilation** refers to the relating of new information to existing schemas, while **accommodation** describes the modification of existing schemas based on new information that a person takes in.

Vygotsky's Sociocultural Theory of Cognitive Development

Lev Vygotsky rejected many of Piaget's ideas, as Vygotsky believed that social interactions between children and others around them play a significant role in their cognitive development.

According to Vygotsky, babies have the elementary mental functions of attention, sensation, perception, and memory. As they interact with others in their environment, babies develop these elementary mental functions into higher mental functions through active, hands-on experiences.

Vygotsky conceptualized a **zone of proximal development**, in which higher mental functions and new learning would be within reach as a child learns from a **more knowledgeable other**. This could be a child's parents, teachers, and others – anyone with a higher level of understanding and ability. In the zone of proximal development, the child is in between the state of not being able to do something and being able to learn how to do it.

According to Vygotsky, the child internalizes the information they take in from their interactions with others. In this way, a child's learning can go beyond their own development as they observe and internalize their learning.

In Vygotsky's theory, language is the means by which the more knowledgeable other transmits information to the child. Thus, in Vygotsky's view, learning involves cooperation and collaborative dialogue, which promotes the development of language (including private speech and internal speech), and therefore the child's cognitive development.

Kohlberg's Stages of Moral Development

According to Kohlberg, moral development is a process that parallels a child's process of cognitive development. He viewed moral development as occurring through 3 levels, each of which is composed of 2 stages.

The first level is **pre-conventional**, which describes the moral reasoning of elementary school aged children (up to the age of 9 years). In the first stage of pre-conventional moral development, the child obeys the authority figure because they fear punishment. In the second stage, the child follows rules in order to be rewarded for doing so. In other words, moral behavior is based on the child's own self-interest.

The next level is **conventional** morality, which begins in early adolescence. The initial stage of conventional morality involves actions seeking to gain approval from others. This is often described as seeking to be a "good boy" or "good girl." In the following stage, the adolescent is focused on obeying laws and following the rules, in order to avoid guilt and disapproval.

Finally, in **post-conventional** morality, the focus is on going beyond the rules and developing one's own sense of what is right. In the initial stage of post-conventional morality, the adult is concerned for individual rights and being a moral person. In the following stage, the person is guided by their own individual moral principles, which are derived from larger, universal moral ideas. However, many adults never reach this stage.

Gilligan's Ethics of Care

Kohlberg's research on moral development was based on research studies with male participants. Carol Gilligan, who had worked with Kohlberg during that time, published her critique of his research as well as her own theories of moral development from a feminist perspective.

Because of gender-based differences in socialization, men are more likely to value principles of justice and rights, while women are more likely to value care and relationships. According to Gilligan, people make moral decisions based on how their actions will impact others. Gilligan found that this approach is typically associated with women, based on their socialization, but that it holds true for men as well.

Gilligan noted that, while men's moral judgments were based primarily on beliefs of justice, women's moral judgments were based on **ethics of care**. Further, while Kohlberg had conceptualized the transitions between stages as increases in cognitive capability as an individual grows older, Gilligan instead conceptualized these transitions as based on changes in a woman's sense of self, without specified age ranges.

Gilligan's stages of the ethics of care follow the same terminology as Kohlberg's levels of moral development: pre-conventional, conventional, and post-conventional morality.

In Gilligan's theory, **preconventional morality is** based on survival needs. In this stage, the individual bases their moral decisions on their own needs before considering the needs of others.

The next stage is **conventional morality**, which is based on self-sacrifice. While transitioning into this stage, women begin to emphasize the importance of relationships and focus on caring for the needs of others. In this stage, the individual sees the good in sacrifice, putting others' needs ahead of their own. Society reinforces women's selfless actions, in which they are most responsive to the needs of others.

As women move from conventional morality into **post-conventional morality**, they shift from wanting to be "good" to wanting to follow their own beliefs. Post-conventional morality is defined by integrated care, basing moral decisions on the woman's own beliefs and what is true for her.

While Kohlberg's stages view men as reaching higher stages that women did not often reach, leading to a view of women as inferior, Gilligan's theory instead positions women as often reaching the highest level of post-conventional morality.

Psychodynamic Theories

Psychodynamic theories include Freudian and ego psychology perspectives, but also include newer perspectives of personality development and understandings of human problems in living. Social workers' use of psychodynamic theories include **psychoanalytic (drive) theory**, **ego psychology**, **object relations**, and **self psychology**.

The earliest and perhaps the most well known of the psychodynamic theories is Sigmund Freud's psychoanalytic theory, also known as drive theory. If Freud's theory seems outdated, that is because it is. Even so, it has been especially impactful and is still important because of the many newer theories that it helped to inspire.

In Freud's view, personality develops primarily in childhood, with early childhood experiences having an especially significant impact. According to Freud's psychoanalytic theory of psychosexual development, individuals process through the following stages:

Freud's Stages of Psychosexual Development

Oral Stage (Birth to 18 months)

During the **oral stage**, the infant seeks gratification through stimulation from the mouth, such as through breastfeeding. As the infant progresses through this stage, they become less dependent on caregivers to have their basic needs met.

Anal Stage (18 months to 3 years)

The **anal stage** takes place between the ages of 18 months to 3 years. During this age range, toilet training takes place, and so Freud conceived of pleasure as being derived through the control of bowel and bladder movement. Gratification in this stage is therefore focused on the anus and bladder.

Phallic Stage (3 to 6 years)

During the **phallic stage**, children become aware of their bodies, and Freud conceptualized the libido as becoming focused on the genitalia. Children learn the physical differences between the sexes as well as differences between genders. In this stage, Freud believed, a boy engages in competition with his father for possession of the mother, and described this as the **Oedipus complex**. Similarly, Freud described girls as competing with the mothers for possession of the father, and he called this the **Electra complex**.

Latency Stage (7 years until puberty)

Children in the latency stage, Freud believed, begin to identity with their same sex parent. During this time, as children are focused on school and other activities, energy is directed into developing the self. Sexual and aggressive drives are expressed in more socially acceptable ways using the defenses of repression and sublimation.

Genital Stage (Puberty through adult life)

During puberty, adolescents enter the genital stage. During the genital stage, the start of puberty brings an active libido and a reawakening of sexual attraction. Freud theorized the source of pleasure in this stage as heterosexual relationships and sexual intercourse. A fixation at this stage, Freud believed, could lead to "perversions" that prevent healthy sexual relationships.

Structural Theory

Freud's **structural theory** proposed three internal structures that guide personality functioning: the **id**, the **ego**, and the **superego**. According to Freud, the id is the source of an individual's primitive drives and instincts, driven by the **pleasure principle**. The ego mediates between the drives and external reality, moderates conflict between the drives and the individual's sense of prohibitions, and serves to adapt the individual to external reality. The superego, also considered the ego ideal, is a critical and moralizing part of the self and the source of an individual's conscience. Working together, these three components create the complexity of human behavior and experience.

Freud also describes three levels of the mind: the **conscious**, the **pre-conscious**, and the **unconscious**. The conscious mind includes mental activities and states of which individuals are aware. The pre-conscious refers to thoughts, feelings, desires, and memories of which the individual is not aware, but that can be brought to awareness relatively easily. The unconscious mind involves thoughts, feelings, desires, and memories of which the person is unaware. The word **subconscious** is sometimes used to refer to the pre-conscious mind, and, less often, may also be used to refer to the unconscious mind.

Neurosis

According to psychoanalytic theory, **neurosis** is a chronic state of fear or anxiety that causes distress and difficulty in functioning, but does not result in delusions, hallucinations, or other difficulties in reality testing. Neurosis describes a wide range of symptoms and is distinct from psychosis.

Psychological Defense Mechanisms

Defense mechanisms are ways that people protect themselves from unpleasant thoughts, feelings, and behaviors. For the most part, these are unconscious processes, as individuals use defense mechanisms without realizing that they are doing so. These defenses distort one's reality even as they serve a protective function. Defense mechanisms are sometimes called coping mechanisms, as they help us to cope with challenging emotions and experiences. However, coping mechanisms and coping strategies are also terms that may refer to conscious, voluntary processes.

Compensation involves efforts to make up for an actual or perceived deficit. For example, if a high school student is having difficulty academically, they may devote extra time to practicing sports so that they can excel in that area. Compensation may also be referred to as **overcompensation**.

Conversion is the expression of repressed emotion through bodily experiences or disruptions. For example, a student who feels anxious about an exam may develop stomach pains or nausea.

Denial is the inability to acknowledge a feeling, event, or experience due to the blocking of that experience from conscious awareness. For example, a client who drinks alcohol all day and does not engage in social relationships or productive activities may experience denial with regard to the problematic nature of their alcohol use.

Devaluation is the characterizing of oneself, another person, or an object as completely flawed or worthless, or the exaggeration of that person or object's negative characteristics. Devaluation, along with idealization, is a component of splitting.

Displacement is the transfer of negative emotions directed at one target to an unrelated person, animal, or object. For example, a person who has a difficult day at work may be angry with a co-worker, but not able to express this anger to the co-worker without negative consequences at work. Instead, they come home and yell at their dog and their partner. Displacement is commonly described as "taking it out on" someone when one is upset about something.

Dissociation is the loss of connection to present experience. A person may feel as though they are watching their life from the outside, separated from the self and from the reality of the moment.

For example, a person who experiences a traumatic event may have no memory of what they experienced if they experienced dissociation at the time the event took place.

Idealization is a component of splitting. When a person idealizes, they attribute overly positive qualities to another person or object. They may view that person or object as perfect, or as having extreme positive qualities. Individuals with borderline personality disorder often alternate between idealization and devaluation.

Identification is similar to introjection, which is described below, but goes further in that the individual *identifies* with the source of introjected beliefs in ways that go beyond those particular beliefs. For example, a husband may expect his wife to do all of the housework because he sees himself in the same role that his father was in, as a head of household in a family that maintained the stereotypical gender roles of that time.

Identification with the aggressor is the process by which a victim of abuse or aggression becomes aggressive toward others. For example, a child may experience abuse at home, and then come to school and act out the role of the abusive parent by bullying other students.

Incorporation is the taking in (sometimes referred to as mentally *ingesting*) of another person or parts of a person and *incorporating* them into the self. Incorporation is associated with the oral stage and can be considered an early form of introjection and identification.

Introjection, or **internalization**, is the adoption of others' values and beliefs as one's own. For example, a young child is likely to internalize their parents' values, norms, and ways of seeing the world.

Intellectualization is the process by which a person separates the content of an experience from the emotions associated with that experience. For example, a person diagnosed with an early stage of cancer and whose doctor recommends watchful waiting may spend many hours researching treatment options without being aware of their feelings about having a cancer diagnosis.

Isolation of affect is the separation of painful emotions from an event, even as an individual is able to recall and describe the event. For example, a person may get fired from their job, which they depend on financially, but state "it doesn't matter, it makes no difference to me."

Passive aggression is the expression of negative feelings in an indirect manner. For example, a person who is angry with a friend about something the friend said may not confront the friend directly, but instead ignore messages and show up late to see this friend.

Projection is a defense mechanism in which a person recognizes their undesired or socially unacceptable traits or impulses in another person, even if the other person is not actually displaying those traits or impulses. Memory tip: Think of a film projector *projecting* the feelings of movie actors onto a screen.

Projective identification is the experiencing of others' projections as reflections of oneself. For example, in working with a client who projects negative traits onto the therapist, the therapist may see themself as possessing (i.e., the therapist comes to identify with) those traits.

Rationalization is the attempt to justify or excuse one's actions. For example, a student who cheats on an exam may tell himself that getting higher grades will help him to become successful so that he can support his family and have a positive impact in the world.

Reaction formation is behaving outwardly in a way that portrays the opposite of one's inner emotions. Reaction formation functions to replace an unacceptable feeling or impulse with its opposite. For example, a person who is furious with his spouse may bring home flowers.

Regression is an individual's returning to behaviors associated with an earlier stage of development. For example, an adolescent who is facing heightened stressors may experience bedwetting.

Repression is the removal of painful memories, thoughts, and feelings from conscious awareness. For example, an individual who suffers a sudden tragic loss of a family member may not consciously remember that the person has died.

Splitting is an all or nothing approach in which an individual fails to notice both the positive and negative aspects of another, and instead uses idealization and devaluation. The defense of splitting is commonly used in individuals with borderline personality disorder. Because the person is unable to integrate others' positive and negative traits, splitting serves to protect their experience of good in themself and others.

Sublimation is the redirecting of otherwise unacceptable emotions or harmful urges into a healthier, more acceptable outlet. For example, a child who has been getting into fights due to difficulty managing aggression may join a martial arts club. Social workers can encourage clients to channel their emotions in positive and productive ways based on an understanding of sublimation.

Substitution is the replacement of a goal that is unattainable or unacceptable with a more attainable or acceptable one. For example, an athlete who initially desires to compete in the Olympics but cannot reach that goal may instead try out for a local neighborhood sports team.

Symbolization is a defense mechanism in which a person comes to see one object or idea as representing another.

Turning against the self is the deflection of aggressive or otherwise unacceptable impulses from an external target toward oneself.

Undoing is an effort to take back the effects of a behavior that goes against one's morals or values. For example, in Shakespeare's *Macbeth*, Lady Macbeth seeks to rid herself of guilt for her role in Duncan's murder by compulsively washing what she imagines to be blood off of her hands.

Object Relations Theory and Self-Psychology

Object relations theory and **self psychology** are both biopsychosocial theories that address the ways in which a person's interactions with their environment shape their development and behavior.

Object Relations Theory

While Freudian theory was focused on biological instincts as the factors impacting personality, object relations theory instead looks at the impact of interpersonal relationships on human development. People are impacted by their relationships with others as well as by their internal images and representations of themselves and others. According to object relations theory, early interactions between infants and their caregivers shape the infant's attitude toward self and others, relational patterns, and defenses.

A key object relations theorist was Margaret Mahler. According to Mahler, key experiences in object relations are attachment, separation/individuation, rapprochement, and the development of object constancy.

Attachment, in object relations, describes an affectional tie between one person and another specific individual. These attachments occur at all ages, may be formed with multiple people, and tend to persist over time.

Separation/individuation leads to the development of the individual's ego structure as the individual internalizes representations of the self and of others.

Rapprochement is a sub-phase of separation/individuation, and describes the process of a child actively returning to their caregiver as they also become aware of their separateness from the caregiver. The child demonstrates their needs for both autonomy and support.

Object constancy is an individual's ability to believe in the stability and intactness of a relationship, even during periods of distance or conflict.

Self Psychology

Self psychology, a theory initially developed by Kohut, places the individual at the center of their own developmental process. According to self psychology, infants are born with an innate capacity to develop. Through the responsiveness of the caretaking environment, they develop a strong sense of self.

Behavioral Theories

Behavioral theories view human behavior as being determined by stimuli in the person's environment. As the environment changes, an individual's personality can evolve across the entire lifespan.

Conditioning, in the context of behavioral theories, refers to learning. Two key models of conditioning are **classical conditioning** and **operant conditioning.**

Classical Conditioning

Classical conditioning is based on the work of Ivan Pavlov. If you have heard of Pavlov's dogs, you may be familiar with this model. In classical conditioning, learning happens when a previously neutral stimulus is *paired* with an unconditioned, or involuntary stimulus. Through conditioning, the previously neutral stimulus becomes conditioned. That is, it comes to elicit the same response that the unconditioned stimulus elicits involuntarily.

There are many terms to know when it comes to classical conditioning. Here are the main concepts of this model:

An **unconditioned stimulus** elicits an unconditioned response. That is, it triggers a response involuntarily without any learning required.

The **unconditioned response** is the automatic response to the unconditioned stimulus.

Unconditioned, then, means that the person responds naturally to this stimulus (i.e., they did not learn to do so).

A neutral stimulus does not elicit a response, but when immediately followed by an unconditioned stimulus in repeated trials, becomes paired with that unconditioned stimulus. It then, through learning, becomes a **conditioned stimulus** and elicits a **conditioned response.** This is the process of classical conditioning.

A **conditioned stimulus** is a stimulus that the individual has learned (i.e., been conditioned) to respond to. That is, the person has been conditioned to respond to this stimulus in a particular way.

A **conditioned response** is the response that the individual has learned, through conditioning, to a conditioned stimulus.

Operant Conditioning

Operant conditioning, based on the work of Edward Thorndike and later B. F. Skinner, is a system of learning based on the idea that we can increase or decrease the frequency of a behavior by following it with a consequence. This consequence can be an addition or withdrawal of a stimulus. From this perspective, there is no free will, as human behavior is either random or is in response to environmental conditioning.

Here are some key terms to know when it comes to operant conditioning. Note that adding a stimulus is referred to as "positive," while withdrawing a stimulus is referred to as "negative." If that addition or withdrawal of a stimulus increases a behavior, it is functioning as reinforcement. If, on the other hand, the addition or withdrawal of a stimulus decreases a behavior, it is functioning as punishment.

Positive reinforcement is the addition of a consequence (a resulting event that is, in this case, a reward) when that addition increases a behavior. For example, if you give yourself a scoop of ice cream after studying for an hour to support yourself in continuing to study, and it works in getting you to keep studying, that would be positive reinforcement. You have added the stimulus of ice cream and it is increasing the desired behavior of studying.

Negative reinforcement is the removal of a stimulus when that removal increases a behavior. For example, if your partner agrees to do the dishes each evening when you study so that you don't have to, and that motivates you to keep studying, that would be negative reinforcement. Your partner has removed the stimulus of having to do the dishes, and this has increased the desired behavior of studying.

Positive punishment is the addition of a stimulus that decreases a behavior. Don't try this at home, but let's say you set your phone to give you an electric shock anytime you pick it up to browse social media during your studying time. If the electric shock decreases your social media use, that would be an example of positive punishment.

Negative punishment is the removal of a stimulus when that removal decreases a behavior. For example, let's say a child talks out of turn at school and is given detention. Having to sit in detention is the addition of a stimulus, and, if effective, it will decrease the undesired behavior of talking out of turn and function as a form of negative punishment.

Shaping is the continuous reinforcement of successive approximations of the target behavior. In other words, it would not make sense to wait to reinforce a perfect behavior that a person has not yet learned. How will they learn what to do? Instead, one can reinforce the person's development of behavior as it gets closer and closer to the desired behavior.

Extinction is the ending of a learned behavior, which occurs through the removal of the consequence. A conditioned stimulus is presented without the unconditioned stimulus enough times that it no longer elicits the conditioned response.

Fowler's Stages of Faith Development

Fowler saw faith as a virtue that completes a person, and conceptualized the stages of faith development as defining a person's life journey. However, according to his theory, most people remain at the intermediate stages, with few making it to the highest stages of faith development.

Stage 0: Primal, or undifferentiated faith

In this pre-stage, infants realize that they are separate beings from their parents, but do not conceptualize the difference between what is real and what is imaginary. Even so, as they begin to trust others, they develop early conceptions of faith.

Stage 1: Intuitive-projective faith

In early childhood, language and communication skills begin to develop. Highly influenced by their parents, children can begin to develop vague ideas of a God that is magical in nature.

Stage 2: Mythic-literal faith

In this stage of middle childhood, children take literally the religious stories that they hear from those around them. They conceptualize God as having a physical form.

Stage 3: Synthetic-conventional faith

In this stage, individuals are exposed to different forms of faith, and begin to develop their own belief systems. However, individuals tend to establish their beliefs without flexibility, and without realizing that they hold a particular system of belief.

Stage 4: Individuative-reflective faith

In this stage, the individual can critically examine their beliefs. They realize they have been operating within a particular system of belief, and that there are other systems of belief around them as well.

Stage 5: Conjunctive faith

In the conjunctive faith stage, associated with middle adulthood, individuals seek multiple interpretations of reality. They begin to see life as mysterious, and take an accepting and explorational stance. They seek out various ideologies and explore beyond their own belief system.

Stage 6: Universalizing faith

In this final stage, which few people ever reach, individuals challenge the existing social order. They dedicate their lives to serving others, as they see this service as their duty.

Resiliency Theory

Resiliency theory helps us understand how and why people survive and thrive despite experiencing incredible adversity and risk. **Resiliency**, also called **resilience**, provides a theoretical basis for strengths-based approaches. In addition to considering risk factors, social workers should consider protective factors that support client resilience. Protective factors are found not only in the individual but also in the community.

The concept of resilience involves an individual or community's ability to overcome difficult experiences and risks in order to "bounce back" and adapt to challenging circumstances. Resilience at the individual level is associated with coping, self-efficacy, and competence; it is consistent with a social work strengths perspective. Community resilience, similarly, refers to the process of coping and recovery in communities faced with collective stress and trauma.

Maslow's Hierarchy of Needs

Abraham Maslow's **need theory of motivation** provides an important model for meeting clients where they are and prioritizing their basic needs. The first four levels are the needs that Maslow describes as **deficiency needs**, while Maslow separates out the final level and describes it as consisting of **growth needs**.

Physiological Needs

According to Maslow, the foundation of human needs consists of **physiological needs**. Physiological needs include food, water, warmth, and rest. Maslow includes sex among this first level of need as well, although this has been controversial.

Safety and Security Needs

Maslow describes the next level of need as **safety and security needs**. We need to be physically secure and protected from threats.

Love and Belongingness Needs

The next level moves from those basic physical and safety needs to **love and belongingness needs.** Love and belongingness needs include friendships as well as romantic relationships. People need to know that they belong, and people need to love and be loved.

Esteem Needs

Next, Maslow describes **esteem needs**. People want to be respected and to feel good about who they are.

Self-Actualization

Finally, apart from the deficiency needs are a person's growth needs, which involve a desire for **self-actualization.** This is a level that most people do not reach. Self-actualization involves living according to out full potential and becoming the most full versions of ourselves

Maslow's theory highlights that, while we cannot live only based on higher-level spiritual or psychological needs, it would not make sense to focus exclusively on physical needs either. In other words, we need to address both our physical needs and our psychological and spiritual needs.

Principles of Human Genetics

Many physical and mental health disorders are, at least in part, inherited. Genes influence factors on a cellular level that play a significant role in determining a person's health and well-being.

Some inherited traits are considered dominant, while others are considered recessive. **Dominant traits** are those that are expressed whether inherited from the genes of one parent or inherited from the genes of both parents. **Recessive traits** are those that may be carried but not expressed when inherited by only one parent, as there would need to be genes for the trait inherited from both parents in order for the person to experience that condition.

Genes may be carried on the sex chromosomes (X or Y), or on the autosomes (non-sex chromosomes). **Autosomal** refers to the carrying of genetic material on a non-sex chromosome; that is, any chromosome other than the X and Y chromosomes.

Epigenetics literally means *above the genome* and refers to the ways in which environmental factors can change how genes are expressed. Because of epigenetics, two identical genomes (such as in the case of identical twins) can be expressed differently. The concept of epigenetics brings together the role of the human genome and the impact of a person's environment. Epigenetics therefore gives us a way to consider the effects of trauma on the body at a cellular level.

Genetic counseling is a specialty health profession that helps patients and families to understand genetic factors contributing to a disease or risk of disease, and to make decisions based on this information. Genetic counselors use the patient's family history as well as genetic testing to inform their assessment.

Gender Identity and Expression

Every person has a gender identity and gender expression. **Gender identity** refers to a person's felt sense of being male, female, non-binary, or any other gender, while biological sex refers to a person's physical traits associated with being male, female, and/or intersex. Gender identity is an aspect of a person's experience whether or not they identify as LGBTQ, and can be the same as, or different from, the person's biological sex. **Gender expression** refers to the ways in which a person demonstrates aspects of their gender identity such as through appearance, clothing, and behavior.

Transgender refers to a person's experience of having a gender identity that is different from the sex that a person was identified with at birth, while **cisgender** refers to a person's experience of having a gender identity that aligns with the sex that the person was identified with at birth. **Sex assigned at birth** is based on physical anatomy and is typically determined before or immediately after birth. The most common sexes assigned at birth are male and female, although intersex is another possible sex at birth.

The term transgender includes people of many genders whose gender identity or expression differs from societal expectations associated with the person's sex assigned at birth. It is an umbrella term that includes people who are transmasculine, transfeminine, non-binary, gender fluid, and agender. Transgender people seek social work services for many of the same reasons that anyone would seek social work services, and may also have social work needs related to transgender identity and gender transition. Because transgender people often experience bullying, isolation, and rejection across micro, mezzo, and macro system levels, community support is often important. Social workers can help clients to access this support.

Intersex Identity

Approximately 1% of individuals are born intersex, with variations in sex based on hormones, chromosomes, and/or anatomy. **Intersex** is an umbrella term that refers to individuals with any of these varying sex characteristics. Controversially, many individuals born intersex are assigned male or female, and many infants with anatomy that is not exclusively male or female are surgically reassigned as female. A growing movement for the rights and acceptance of intersex people seeks to change these practices.

Sexual Orientation

Every person has a sexual orientation. **Sexual orientation** describes a person's attraction toward people who are male, female, and/or any gender identity or expression, or the absence of sexual and/or romantic attration.

With regard to **sexual orientation identity development**, gay, lesbian, and bisexual individuals typically experience stages of identity formation as well as stages of coming out to oneself and others. These stages can be broken down into the steps of pre-coming out, coming out, exploration, early relationships, and integration.

There is a broad range of normal sexual orientation identities and sexual behaviors. Some theories describe sexual orientation as determined early in life and remain fixed, while other theories view sexual orientation as fluid.

Even with improvements in society's treatment of LGBTQ people, many queer individuals still experience difficulty with family and community acceptance. In a conservative religious community, for example, queer youth may fear familial rejection as well as the loss of their faith community and friendships if they come out. For those who do not "pass" as heterosexual, coming out may not be experienced as a choice, and harsh treatment by those around them may have an impact even before an individual comes to an understanding of their sexual orientation identity.

Pansexual is a sexual orientation identity defined by a person's sexual and/or romantic attraction to people regardless of sex or gender. Pansexuality is different from **bisexuality** in that the term bisexual often implies attraction to men and women, while pansexual is a label inclusive of more than 2 sexes and genders.

Sexual orientation should be taken into account throughout a person's life course, including in work with older adults.

One particular issue with regard to sexual orientation and gender identity that is relevant to social work practice is the issue of so-called **conversion therapy**. Proponents of conversion therapy claim that it can change a person's sexual orientation from gay or bisexual to heterosexual, or a person's gender identity from transgender to cisgender. Conversion therapy is harmful because it has been found to increase suicidal ideation and other negative mental health outcomes in clients who have been subjected to this pseudoscientific practice. Because of these harms, conversion therapy is considered unethical by all major mental health organizations and has been made illegal in many jurisdictions. Still, the practice remains politically controversial.

Racism and Discrimination

Racism, according to Ibram X. Kendi, "is a marriage of racist policies and racist ideas that produces and normalizes racial inequities." Kendi defines racist policies as measures that produce or sustain racial inequity, while racial inequity describes the status of racial groups that are not given equal status by these policies.

White privilege refers to the unearned and, often, unacknowledged ways in which White people are granted greater access and opportunities than people of color.

Disparate treatment is discriminatory, unfavorable treatment based on an individual's personal characteristics such as age, race, sex, gender identity or expression, sexual orientation, or disability.

Stereotypes are overgeneralized, inaccurate beliefs about members of particular groups, and often target members of marginalized and oppressed groups.

Microaggressions are subtly coded instances of discriminatory acts or speech that target individuals and groups based on race, religion, gender, sexual orientation, class, disability, and other identities. In contrast to overt aggression, microaggressions are thinly veiled and thus often free the perpetrator from accountability. Microaggressions take the form of microassaults, microinsults, and microinvalidations.

Poverty Across Individuals, Families, Groups, Organizations, and Communities

Poverty, often a result of oppression, creates significant problems across all domains of life for individuals, families, groups, organizations, and communities. Social workers should be aware of poverty and its impacts in helping clients to first address basic physiological and safety needs at the individual level as well as systemically.

Asylum Seekers and Refugees

Asylum seekers and refugees are people who flee from their country in order to escape persecution. **Refugees** are considered forced migrants, as they are victims of human rights violations, including war, and cannot return to their previous countries due to the risk of persecution. Refugees who are awaiting an official decision on their refugee status are considered **asylum seekers**.

Praxis: Uniting Theory and Action

Praxis is a term that describes the uniting of theory and action. Praxis refers to action that is based on critical reflection and engagement with theoretical principles. It is a social justice principle advanced by Paulo Freire in his text *Pedagogy of the Oppressed*. Rather than keeping theory within the realm of academia, and real-world practice separate from theoretical work, praxis is an approach that unites the two through reflection.

Cultural Competence in Social Work Practice

Principles of **culturally competent social work practice** include the use of effective interventions grounded in the social worker's commitment to promote social and economic justice with a diverse client population.

Cultural competence requires **cultural humility**, which involves maintaining a stance of "not knowing," continual self-awareness, openness to learning, and a willingness to acknowledge and learn from mistakes.

In culturally competent practice, social workers should work in conjunction with informal support networks within the client's community. It is also important that agency staffing plans reflect the cultural makeup of the client population. In addition, services should be designed in a way that is culturally responsive to the client population.

Anti-Oppression Practice

Anti-oppression practice goes further than cultural competence in that it promotes the dismantling of oppressive systems and the visioning of a new future.

Anti-oppressive social work practice is derived from structural, ecological, and post-modern theories. These theories take into account the fact that individuals may experience target status and/or privilege depending on their different identities.

Both macro and micro social relations are sources of oppression. While oppression resides in societal structures, it is often implemented and enforced by individual interactions and individually reinforced social norms. Clients at all systems levels have experience of both oppression and resistance to that oppression. These experiences are linked to societal issues of politics and policy, and social work exists within that politically charged and contested context. Thus, social work engages with controversial issues and is not politically neutral. Social work is both a caring profession and an active political process, which seeks to transform society to create opportunities for marginalized and oppressed people.

Anti-oppressive practice requires allyship with oppressed groups as well as partnering with social causes and movements.

Social work theory and practice should both be based on the needs and struggles of marginalized and oppressed communities. Social workers should engage with clients, in partnership, to help clients solve problems. In this participatory approach, clients and communities are included and involved in all stages of the change process.

Anti-oppressive practice requires self-reflection and ongoing social analysis on the part of the social worker. Social workers should be aware of power and should utilize power analysis in understanding social issues.

Intersectionality

Intersectionality theory recognizes the ways in which various aspects of identity have combined effects on a person's experiences in life based on the ways in which each identity is associated with oppression and/or privilege.

Environmental Justice

Environmental justice refers to the principle of fair treatment of all people with regard to environmental policies, making sure that no group is forced to bear a disproportionate burden of environmental problems and risks.

Social Determinants of Health

Social determinants of health are conditions in people's living environments that affect a wide range of health, functioning, and quality of life factors. Examples of social determinants of health include racism, discrimination, job opportunities, access to healthy food and exercise, air quality, and water quality. For example, individuals with limited economic resources due to unemployment or low wages are less likely to have access to healthy food, and less likely to have outdoor spaces conducive to physical activity, resulting in higher rates of diabetes. Similarly, when sources of air pollution are located in neighborhoods with low-income residents, those residents are likely to have higher rates of asthma as a result.

Feminist Theories

Feminist theories address specific issues and understandings relevant to women, seek to explain differences between men's and women's experiences, and seek to increase awareness of the oppression of women. Feminist theories acknowledge the gendered aspects of social problems as well as the gendered aspects of care.

Feminist social work seeks to end **patriarchy**, which is a system in which men hold the power in society and women are excluded from that power. Feminist social work further seeks to empower women and to raise public consciousness regarding gender inequity.

Conflict Theory

According to **conflict theory**, which originates in the work of Karl Marx, conflict between oppressors and oppressed groups happens due to scarcity of resources. In this theory, conflict between oppressive and oppressed groups occurs in a cycle, as some groups dominate others through an unequal division of power. In this model, oppressed groups become alienated from society, and this conflict is a driving force behind social change.

Family Life

The **family life cycle** is a term that describes emotional and intellectual stages that adults pass through in relation to family roles. The stages of the family life cycle begin with *independence* in young adulthood and continue on to *coupling*, or marriage, then to *parenting of babies and children* through to the adolescent years, then to the *launching of adult children*, and finally to *retirement*, or senior adult life. Of course, as with all stage theories, it is important to recognize that these experiences, while common, do not reflect the reality of every person's experience. In particular, these stages may not align with the experiences of LGBTQ people as well as others who do not have children or who are not in long-term, monogamous relationships.

Assessment and Intervention Planning

Social work practice is a broad topic covering both direct practice (interventions to help individuals at the micro level as well as families and small groups at the mezzo level) and indirect practice (interventions to help organizations and communities at the macro level). The term *client* is used inclusively to refer to any individual, family, group, organization, or community that is receiving the help of a social worker.

The early stages of the social work helping process involve engagement, assessment, and intervention planning. In order to help a client or client system, a social worker must establish an alliance and begin to build a relationship based on trust, care, and understanding. The social worker then takes on the role of information gatherer, seeking to understand the client holistically and arrive at a formulation of the client and their presenting problem in the context of their environment and the systems with which they interact. Next, the social worker and client must collaboratively develop a plan for working together in partnership to address the problems for which they are seeking help.

Engagement Phase

The social worker's first task is to engage the client and establish a helping relationship. Effective engagement with clients requires empathy, reflection, and interpersonal skills. During the engagement phase, the social worker seeks to build rapport with the client. Central to engagement is the use of good communication skills, which can be thought of as engaging in person-centered practice. Establishing and building rapport involves attending, active listening, the use of both open- and closed-ended questions, clarification, reflecting back, and validation.

Meeting the Client Where They Are

This is a phrase commonly heard in social work programs, but what does it mean? Meeting the client where they are refers to acknowledging and accepting the client's emotions and life experiences, and working to help the client based on their strengths and present needs. Maslow's hierarchy of needs is a helpful theory for meeting the client where they are. If a person needs help accessing food and shelter, start there. If a person's basic physiological needs are met but they are struggling with self-esteem, focus your assessment and interventions on those needs. *Memory tip: When utilizing MasLOW's hierarchy of needs, focus on the LOWest levels first.*

Validation

One of the most important skills in communication with clients is validation. Validation should be used throughout social work practice, with special attention paid during the engagement phase. Validation is the acknowledgement, without judgment, of a client's experience and emotions as normative and acceptable. Even when some aspects of a person's experience may not appear to be valid, there is always some valid component that the social worker can highlight and reflect back to the client. Focus on validating that which is valid, rather than on invalidating that which does not seem valid.

Unconditional Positive Regard

Carl Rogers, who developed the concept of person-centered therapy (also called client-centered therapy) describes **unconditional positive regard** as caring for and valuing the client as a separate person with their own feelings and experiences.

Accurate Empathic Understanding

Carl Rogers also introduced the concept of **accurate empathic understanding**. Accurate empathic understanding, according to Rogers, is more than a reflection of feelings. It involves an in-the-moment presence and attunement to the client's feelings and experiences.

Anticipatory Empathy

Anticipatory empathy refers to the use of understanding about another person to predict the likely impact of one's words or actions on that other person. Social workers can prepare to enter into a client's world by considering facts about the client's life and using anticipatory empathy to consider the client's likely feelings and experiences.

Acceptance

Similar to unconditional positive regard, acceptance refers to listening, without judgment, and treating the client in a way that is not dependent on the client's thoughts, feelings, behaviors, or personal characteristics.

Verbal and Non-Verbal Communication

The social worker should pay attention to both verbal and non-verbal communication (both theirs and that of the client). In addition to asking questions and reflecting back (paraphrasing), verbal communication includes the use of **minimal encouragers** such as "uh huh," "I see," "right," and "yes." **Non-verbal communication** includes maintaining an appropriate level of eye contact, nodding, and gesturing.

Active Listening

Effective verbal communication between a social worker and client requires active listening. Active listening is important in client engagement, rapport building, and throughout the helping relationship. In addition to listening attentively, active listening requires letting the client know that you are listening and what you have understood. Active listening involves paying attention, listening without interrupting, asking clarifying questions, and reflecting back what you have heard.

Empathic communication is an intentional process of listening, accepting, understanding, and showing care and concern.

Social workers use both open-ended and closed-ended questions in communication with clients. **Open-ended questions** support engagement and exploration, while **closed-ended questions** help to focus the interview to obtain needed information for assessment.

Taking Notes

Social workers sometimes take notes while meeting with a client, in order to ensure that they are gathering the information necessary for assessment and intervention planning. Clients may ask why the social worker is taking notes, and so the social worker should be prepared to explain how the information they are gathering will be used.

Assessment Phase

Having engaged with the client and established a helping relationship, the social worker's next task is assessment. Starting with the client's presenting problem, the social worker diagnoses the problem using social work theories in order to inform the plan that will be developed in collaboration with the client.

Biopsychosocial Assessment

The **biopsychosocial assessment** is a comprehensive, holistic examination of systems that impact a person's functioning. It includes attention to the client's physical health, emotional functioning, social environment, cultural factors, and spiritual or religious beliefs and practices. This assessment may also be referred to as a biopsychosocial-cultural-spiritual assessment.

The use of the biopsychosocial assessment in social work may also be called the **biopsychosocial approach**, as it is the social worker's framework for understanding a client and their presenting problems in the context of their environment and the systems in their lives.

Thinking Ecologically As a Social Worker

Understanding the ecological systems with which humans interact is necessary for both building on human strengths and addressing challenges.

Person-in environment model

Central to social work assessment is the understanding of a person in the context of their environment. The **person-in-environment** perspective considers the individual and their behaviors and experiences in the context of the familial, social, cultural, and political environments in which they live.

Ecological Perspectives

Before the development of ecological systems theory, studies of human development tended to be based on a person in isolation, such as in a laboratory environment. Urie Bronfenbrenner, a psychologist, did not believe that this was a valid method of studying human development, as it placed a research subject, such as a child, in an unfamiliar environment and with an unfamiliar person such as a researcher. Bronfenbrenner was also concerned that social policies related to poverty were not taking a person's surroundings into account. The predominant belief at the time was that poor people were poor because of their biology. For Bronfenbrenner, it was important to look at people in their living environment.

Bronfenbrenner proposed a theory of **human ecology** based on his belief that, in order to help individuals, we need to change the conditions that surround them. Bronfenbrenner proposed that individuals exist in relation to micro, meso, macro, exo, and chronosystems. He used this theory to successfully advocate for the founding of the Head Start program in 1965.

Systems Theory

In social work, individuals should be understood within the context of their social environment. Systems are collections of related parts that function together. A change in one part of a system affects the entire system. A person, individually, is a biological and psychological system, and each person is also a part of family, organizational, community, national, and global systems. Problems in multiple systems may all play a role contributing to the client's presenting problems, and resources across multiple systems can all contribute to the client's strengths and resilience.

Systems theory tells us that people are impacted by, and have an impact upon, the various levels of systems with which they transact. For example, when assessing a client in their environment, it is important to consider family systems, school or work systems, legal systems, and larger social systems.

The **microsystem** refers to the individual and their immediate environment. For example, a child's microsystem may include their parents and siblings, as well as a grandparent who lives in the home.

Mesosystems involve connections between the other people around the individual. For example, the relationship between a child's teachers and that child's parents would be a component of that child's mesosystem.

Exosystems refer to the individual's indirect environment. This includes human relationships that do not involve the individual directly. For example, if a parent has an argument with their boss and loses their job, this will impact the child as an exosystem factor.

The **macrosystem** includes the overarching social and cultural values and norms, as well as policies, that impact all of the other systems. A person of color living in a racist society is impacted negatively by these macrosystem factors.

The **chronosystem** refers to the impact of changes over time. On an individual scale, this might be the impact of a parent's divorce when a child is 4 years old, which would be different from a parent's divorce when that child is 19 years old. On a larger scale, the chronosystem involves the socio-historical context in which a person lives, as well as historical events that impact people differently based on their age at the time of the event.

The Life Model and the Concept of Habitat

In the life model of social work practice, the concept of **habitat** refers to rural or urban environments including residences, workplaces, and public amenities. Based on ecological and life course theories, the life model of social work is an approach that seeks to improve the person-environment fit, particularly with regard to human needs and available resources. Through their impact on person-in-environment transactions, human habitats can support or impede adaptive functioning in families and communities.

Biological Factors in Assessment

In assessing a client's psychosocial needs, it is important to consider biological factors. A person's medical conditions and overall health status will play a significant role in their mental health and overall functioning.

As people mature and age, the body experiences a wide array of changes.

In addition, we should consider the biological impacts of mental states. Mental health problems impact a person's physiology, and physiological conditions impact a person's psychology as well.

The Nervous System

The **central nervous system** consists of the brain and spinal cord. As the *central* part of this system, the brain receives information and coordinates the activities of all parts of the body.

The **autonomic nervous system** functions without conscious involvement (it is *autonomous* and involuntary), and controls the efferent neurons, smooth muscle, cardiac muscle, and gland cells in the body.

Within the autonomic nervous system are 2 sub-systems, the sympathetic nervous system and the parasympathetic nervous system. The **sympathetic nervous system** controls the body's "fight or flight" response. The **parasympathetic nervous system** controls bodily responses of rest and relaxation It relaxes the body after periods of stress and danger. The parasympathetic nervous system is also responsible for some physiological processes such as digestion, and can be thought of as the "rest and digest" system.

Referrals to Physicians

Social workers should clients experiencing signs of a possible medical problem to a physician for a medical evaluation. When a condition may be caused by physical problems, a referral should first be made to determine any medical cause and ensure that the client receives necessary medical treatment. Only once this has been done should the condition be treated in a social work setting.

Assessment Using the *Diagnostic and Statistical Manual of Mental Disorders, 5th edition (DSM-5)*

When assessing psychological factors as part of a biopsychosocial assessment, social workers often use the criteria of the *Diagnostic and Statistical Manual of Mental Disorders, 5th edition (DSM5)*. For specific diagnostic criteria, it is best to consult the DSM directly. If you do not have a printed copy, check to see if your university or public library has it in their e-book collection. You may also have electronic access if your university library subscribes to the Psychiatry Online database.

Below are descriptions of some of the mental health disorders likely to appear on the exam. There are many more disorders, however, which you can find in the DSM along with their diagnostic criteria.

Major Depressive Disorder

Major depressive disorder is diagnosed in clients who have experienced symptoms for a period of 2 weeks or longer. To make a diagnosis of major depressive disorder, the client must experience five or more symptoms during the same 2 week period, including depressed mood or loss of interest or pleasure in all or almost all activities. Other possible symptoms include weight loss or weight gain, slowing down of thought and/or physical movement, fatigue, feelings of worthlessness or inappropriate guilt, difficulty concentrating, and thoughts of death and/or suicidal ideation.

Despite popular belief in a "chemical imbalance" as the cause of depression, the reality of what causes depression is more complex.

Bipolar Disorder

There are two types of bipolar disorder : bipolar I disorder and bipolar II disorder. It is important to be able to distinguish between these two types, as well as to distinguish between major depressive disorder (unipolar depression) and bipolar disorder.

For a diagnosis of **bipolar I disorder**, the client must have experienced at least one manic episode. Most individuals with bipolar I disorder also experience major depressive episodes, but this is not a requirement for the diagnosis.

Bipolar II disorder, on the other hand, is diagnosed based on the presence of at least one major depressive episode and at least one hypomanic episode.

Autism Spectrum Disorder

Autism spectrum disorder is a neurodevelopmental disorder affecting how people communicate, interact, learn, and behave. People with autism spectrum disorder experience difficulties in the areas of social communication and interaction, as well as restricted and repetitive behaviors.

Intellectual Developmental Disorder

Intellectual developmental disorder is also a neuro-developmental disorder, but involves difficulties in general intellectual functioning such as learning, thinking, reasoning, and judgment.

Specific Learning Disorders

Specific learning disorders are characterized by difficulty in reading, writing, and/or mathematics.

Anorexia Nervosa

Anorexia nervosa is an eating disorder in which individuals restrict the types of found and amount of calories that they consume each day. Individuals with anorexia are often concerned with maintaining a low body weight, and may have a distorted body image.

Schizophrenia

Schizophrenia is diagnosed when symptoms consistent with this diagnosis have lasted for 1 month or longer. For a diagnosis of schizophrenia, symptoms must include at least two of these 5 symptoms: delusions, hallucinations, disorganized speech, disorganized or catatonic behavior, or negative symptoms such as diminished emotional expression. At least one of the symptoms must be delusions, hallucinations, or disorganized speech.

Adjustment Disorder

Adjustment disorder involves clinically significant symptoms that occur in response to an identifiable stressor, occur within 3 months of the stressor, have not lasted for more than 6 months following the termination of the stressor and its consequences, and that do not meet criteria for another mental health disorder. The DSM-5 further notes that normal bereavement responses do not meet the criteria for a diagnosis of adjustment disorder.

Gender Dysphoria

Gender dysphoria involves distress related to identifying as a different gender than that assigned to the person at birth. DSM-5 diagnosis requires a component of distress or disability. Therefore, a person's gender identity in and of itself does not constitute a diagnosis of gender dysphoria; the person would only carry this diagnosis if they experience distress or disability related to their gender identity.

Body Dysmorphic Disorder

Body dysmorphic disorder is a mental condition in which the individual is distressed by obsessive thoughts about one or more perceived flaws or defects in their physical appearance that are not apparent to others, or that would appear only slight to others.

Conversion Disorder

Conversion disorder, also known as functional neurological symptom disorder, is a mental health disorder in which the individual experiences altered voluntary motor or sensory function, which cannot be explained by any medical condition. For a diagnosis of conversion disorder, it is necessary for the client to be assessed to rule out neurological disease

Somatic Symptom Disorder

Somatic symptom disorder is defined by the distress or preoccupation that a person experiences based on physical symptoms, even as it is also a condition that involves physical symptoms for which no medical cause can be found. Somatic symptom disorder is characterized by a person's high level of focus on physical symptoms, and emotional distress that the person experiences related to their preoccupation with their symptoms.

Factitious Disorder

Factitious disorder is a mental health condition in which a person deceives other people by appearing sick, purposefully becoming sick, or injuring oneself. Factitious disorder is distinguished from malingering by the fact that those with factitious disorder do not receive clear external rewards in relation to their symptoms. With **malingering**, on the other hand, clients seek to achieve a specific goal such as financial gain, excusal from work, or to address legal issues. While factitious disorder is a DSM-5 mental disorder, malingering is not, but is instead listed as a condition that may be a focus of clinical attention.

Persistent Complex Bereavement Disorder

Persistent complex bereavement disorder is diagnosed only after 12 months have passed in adults, or 6 months in children, since the death of someone with whom the bereaved person had a close relationship. This time frame is intended to distinguish between normal grief and persistent grief.

Personality Disorders

Personality disorders involve ways of thinking, feeling, and behaving that negatively impact a person's functioning in significant ways. These ways of thinking, feeling, and behaving endure for a long period of time and impact many areas of a person's life.

Borderline Personality Disorder

Borderline personality disorder, also known as BPD, a mental health disorder that involves instability in mood, behavior, and overall functioning. Because of the person's unstable emotions, they often act impulsively and have chaotic interpersonal relationships. Individuals with borderline personality disorder often describe feelings of emptiness and a fear of abandonment. Borderline personality disorder is treated with evidence-based practices including dialectical behavior therapy (DBT) and mentalization-based treatment (MBT).

While there is significant stigma about all mental health and substance use disorders, there is particular stigma around the diagnosis of borderline personality disorder as it is sometimes used as a pejorative label. While the diagnosis can in many cases be helpful and even at times validating, as it can explain a person's experiences, the diagnosis can also be experienced as hurtful or invalidating.

Narcissistic Personality Disorder

Individuals with **narcissistic personality disorder** display exaggerated feelings of self-importance even as they also experience low self-esteem. Narcissistic personality disorder is characterized by a sense of entitlement, a need for constant admiration, and the exaggeration of achievements and abilities. Individuals with narcissistic personality disorder have significant interpersonal difficulties and have difficulty regulating their emotions and behavior. Treatment options for narcissistic personality disorder include mentalization based treatment, schema focused psychotherapy, and transference-focused psychotherapy.

Histrionic Personality Disorder

Histrionic personality disorder is a mental health disorder in which the person exhibits dramatic behavior and experiences an overwhelming desire to be noticed, recognized, and appreciated. For individuals with histrionic personality disorder, attention seeking behaviors typically begin in early childhood. Individuals may exhibit inappropriate seductive behaviors, and often experience a strong desire for the approval of others. This may be caused by a distorted self-image and low self-worth. For people with histrionic personality disorder, treatment may involve various types of therapy including psychodynamic psychotherapy, cognitive-behavioral therapy (CBT), and interpersonal therapy (IPT).

Antisocial Personality Disorder

Individuals with antisocial personality disorder show no respect for the rights of others. They have a demonstrated history of impulsive, aggressive, and violent behavior, including evidence of conduct disorder beginning in adolescence. This is very different from the common, popular usage of the word "antisocial" when referring to someone who is actually asocial and avoids social interaction.

Obsessive-Compulsive Personality Disorder

Obsessive-compulsive personality disorder (OCPD) is different from obsessive-compulsive disorder (OCD) in that OCPD has an overall focus on control, order and perfection rather than on specific obsessive thoughts or compulsive behaviors

A Note on Normal Grief and Loss

Uncomplicated bereavement is listed in the DSM-5 as a condition (but not a disorder) that may be a focus of clinical attention. Uncomplicated bereavement is defined as a normal reaction to the death of a loved one, which may include symptoms that would otherwise indicate a major depressive episode. In uncomplicated bereavement, it is normal to experience sadness, insomnia, low appetite, and weight loss. Individuals may seek (and receive) treatment for these symptoms even when they do not meet criteria for major depressive disorder.

Suicide Risk Assessment

In assessing a client's mental health, attention must be paid to **suicide risk assessment**. Social workers should consider a client's risk factors, as well as any verbal statements that may imply suicidal ideation, to determine the client's risk and conduct safety planning if appropriate.

Risk factors for suicide include previous suicide attempts, a history of depression or other mental disorders, serious illness and chronic pain, criminal or other legal problems, job loss or other financial problems, impulsivity or aggression, substance use, and adverse childhood experiences. LGBTQ individuals, and in particular transgender people, also experience higher rates of suicide.

Social, Cultural, and Spiritual Factors

In assessment and intervention planning, it is important to understand a client's **support system**. This can include biological family, family of choice, friends, acquaintances, groups, and organizations. Family members may include a spouse or partner of any gender, as well as children, parents, grandparents, and other extended family.

Social factors also include macro-level issues that impact people's lives such as poverty, homelessness, and pervasive forms of discrimination and oppression. People are impacted by structural inequities, marginalization, and oppression including racism, sexism, transphobia, homophobia, ageism, and ableism.

When considering social factors, it is important to also consider factors related both to the natural environment and to the built environment.

Social workers must be sensitive to the impact of **culture** on how clients experience and make sense of the world around them and their place in it. Culture includes race and ethnicity but can also involve other communities with which a client may identify based on religion, gender, sexual orientation, political affiliation, personal interests, and more.

Spirituality generally has a positive impact on a person's health and well-being. Spiritual factors covered in an assessment include spiritual beliefs; faith-based activities in which the person engages; the person's involvement, if any, in organized religion; the person's spiritual or worship practices; and the resources that the person can draw upon based on their spirituality or religion.

The Stress-Diathesis Model

The **stress-diathesis model** represents a theory of dynamic exchange between a person's genes, their environment, and human behavior. While a person may have a genetic predisposition to mental health disorders, a person's environment (such as exposure to significant stressors) affects the expression of these genes. At the biological level, this has been studied through evaluation of the effects of the stress hormone cortisol. Thus, in the stress-diathesis model, mental health disorders are not considered to be caused exclusively by either the person's genetics or their environment, but rather by the interactions between both of these factors.

Components of a Mental Status Exam

While a **mental status exam** does not lead directly to a DSM-5 diagnosis, it is still an important assessment tool. You can think of a mental status exam as the psychiatric equivalent of a physical exam. A mental status examination is a standard tool that clinicians use to assess a client's cognitive and behavioral functioning. Components of the mental status examination include appearance, behavior, speech, mood, affect, perception, thought content, thought process, insight, judgment, and cognition.

Distinguishing Between Mood and Affect

Mood, as a component of the mental status exam, refers to a person's subjective experience of their own feeling state. In a mental status exam, the clinician will typically ask the client how they are feeling and quote this description verbatim as the client's mood. While mood refers to the person's internal experience, **affect** describes how a person's mood appears to others

Collateral Contact

Communication with outside sources of information, such as family members as well as other treatment providers, with appropriate client consent, can be an important aspect of client assessment. Using collateral information as part of the assessment is consistent with systems theory and the person-in-environment perspective. Collateral contacts can be a resource as the social worker and client collaborate on assessment and treatment.

Addiction and the Stages of Change

Assessment of clients with substance related and addictive disorders often involves use of the transtheoretical model of change, which posits that individuals with addiction progress through stages of change with regard to their readiness to pursue treatment and recovery.

Transtheoretical Stages of Change Model

Even if you do not work in a substance abuse treatment setting, it is still important to understand client readiness to change. The most common model for assessing readiness to change is the **transtheoretical stages of change model**, which consists of the following stages: precontemplation, contemplation, preparation, action, and maintenance. Relapse is often a part of the recovery process as well. A client may need to progress through these stages several times before they achieve long-term recovery.

Pre-contemplation refers to a stage in which the person is not yet ready or willing to change. The person may be in denial about the need for change, or they may feel demoralized due to multiple unsuccessful attempts at change. The person may also not be informed about the consequences of their behavior. The social work role during this stage is to educate the client about the consequences of their behavior and help the client to evaluate the pros and cons of changing the behavior.

During the **contemplation** stage, the client has acknowledged a desire to change without a specific commitment. The client may see the need to change a behavior but may still be working through the pros and cons. In this stage, the social worker can help the client articulate their reasons why they desire to change, and help the client begin to make a plan.

The **preparation** stage is defined by the client's readiness and willingness to work toward change. In this stage, the client begins to take some small steps in working toward their goal. The social worker, in this stage, helps the client to begin taking those steps toward the goal.

Clients in the **action** stage are actively changing their behavior. During this stage, clients have recently made a change and intend to continue with that change. This may involve reducing or eliminating a problematic behavior, and/or developing new, healthy behaviors. In the action stage, the social worker helps the client to track their progress and to maintain their commitment. The social worker may support and cheerlead the client for their progress, and help the client to see the benefits of the change they are making.

Once clients have reached **maintenance**, they have successfully implemented the desired behavioral change and are working to continue with that change. In the maintenance stage, it is important to work on relapse prevention. When working with clients in the maintenance stage, social workers continue to support and encourage the client in maintaining their new behavior. The social worker can provide accountability and skills to help the client prevent relapse.

Relapse is a very common and normal part of the change process. The term relapse refers to an event or period in which the client does not maintain the desired behavior and instead returns to the previous behavior that they had worked to change. The social worker should normalize the experience of relapse and provide psychoeducation on the stages of change. The social worker can also help the client understand what led to the relapse and help the client to return to the change process.

Dual Diagnosis

Dual diagnosis refers to the assessment and treatment of clients who meet criteria for one or more substance related and addictive disorders as well as one or more mental health disorders. For example, a client may have both cocaine addiction and bipolar disorder.

Gambling Addiction

Gambling addiction, as with other addictions, can be destructive for the person with addiction as well as for their family. Gambling addiction requires specialized treatment to address the behavioral chain of events leading to problematic behavior as well as its underlying causes.

Internet Gaming Addiction

Social workers are likely to encounter clients of all ages and genders whose involvement with internet gaming creates problems in functioning. According to the DSM-5, this is an area under further study.

Intervention Methods and Theories

Social workers practice in a wide range of settings and help clients and client systems with increasingly complex problems. In addition to providing clients with the common factors of a therapeutic or helping relationship, social workers must also possess technical expertise in order to help clients through skillful and effective interventions.

Social work with individuals and families is referred to as micro practice, direct practice, or clinical practice. Social work interventions are focused on identifying strengths and facilitating client empowerment.

Social Work Interventions Across Client Systems

A Focus on Empowerment

Empowerment practices, based on empowerment theory, focus on power in order to reduce inequity and support equity. Empowerment is used to counteract experiences of powerlessness by positioning marginalized people as the experts of their own experience. In social work practice, empowerment involves collaborating with clients to develop solutions and connecting clients to community resources.

The Strengths Perspective

A key aspect of social work intervention across all client systems is the **strengths perspective**. In using the strengths perspective, the social worker should identify the client's internal and external resources in order to support resilience. The strengths perspective does not focus on targeting specific symptoms but rather focuses on client assets or strengths.

The Social Work Helping Relationship

Central to all social work interventions is the **social worker-client relationship**. By attending to the needs of the client during the engagement and assessment phases, social workers build rapport and establish a therapeutic alliance. This underlying work towards a helping relationship is critical to the success of the intervention phase.

Interview Principles and Techniques

One of the most important social work tools is the **interview**, which is an intentional conversation used to engage, assess, plan, and intervene at all levels of social work practice. Interview techniques include supporting, clarifying, focusing, confronting, validating, providing feedback, and redirecting when needed.

Supporting techniques involve active listening, as well as the use of reflection and validation. **Clarifying techniques** involve the use of both open-ended and closed-ended questions to ask the client for details about their feelings and experiences.

Prevention Strategies

Rather than only intervening after a problem has developed, it is better to prevent problems in the first place. **Prevention** is a public health concept that refers to interventions used to reduce or eliminate social, psychological, or other factors that cause and contribute toward health problems, mental health problems, and socio-economic problems. Prevention can be considered in terms of *primary*, *secondary*, and *tertiary* prevention strategies:

Primary prevention refers to interventions that seek to protect the public from contracting an illness, developing an injury, or engaging in an unhealthy or high-risk behavior. The focus is on reducing risk factors for illness and injury. For example, influenza vaccines provided to an entire community would be an example of primary prevention. Primary prevention seeks to support the community *before* a problem develops, and typically happens on a large scale. It is considered to be the most cost-effective form of prevention.

Secondary prevention involves the use of interventions to prevent further complications or harm in individuals already affected by an illness or injury. The focus is on avoiding escalation of a problem as well as containing that problem. For example, a person who tests positive for COVID-19 may be given an antiviral medication to reduce symptoms and prevent the need for hospitalization.

Tertiary prevention strategies help people to manage long-term problems while preventing further worsening and maximizing the person's quality of life. Often, tertiary prevention requires an individualized approach in order to help clients manage complex and long-term conditions.

Social Work Practice with Individuals

Social workers practicing with individuals typically take on the role of a caseworker or psychotherapist. Social work practice with individuals can take place in a variety of settings including agencies, schools, hospitals, and private practice.

It is common for social workers in healthcare settings to work as members of interdisciplinary teams, as the field moves toward the integration of medical and behavioral healthcare services. School social workers also commonly work on interdisciplinary teams alongside educators and other service providers.

When providing psychotherapy, social workers must take care to not label diversity as pathological.

Psychotherapy Theories and Models

Psychotherapy can take the form of **long-term treatment** or **short-term treatment**. Even treatment that a social worker intends to be long-term can become short-term, as clients may decide to end treatment early. Clients do not always want long-term, open-ended treatment, and significant benefits can often be achieved through short-term treatment. Short-term treatment tends to focus more on here-and-now problems.

One clinical advantage of short-term treatment as compared to long-term treatment is that having a known termination date can motivate both the client and the social worker to mobilize their available resources in order to reach the client's goals. Both short-term and long-term models can include the use of evidence-based practice interventions and can be effective. While insurance plans may at times seek to limit the number of sessions a client can receive, parity laws require insurance plans that cover mental health services to cover such services to the same extent that they cover physical health services, without any treatment limitations that are more restrictive than those placed on physical health services.

Psychodynamic Psychotherapy

Psychodynamic psychotherapy approaches explore early childhood experiences and seek to understand their contribution to adult problems in functioning. From a psychodynamic perspective, the client's presenting problems are seen as stemming from long-standing personality traits and patterns. In psychodynamic psychotherapy, the clinician is likely to use techniques of interpretation and confrontation to bring unconscious processes to the client's conscious awareness. Psychodynamic psychotherapy is often long-term and open-ended, but can be provided on a short-term basis as well.

Cognitive Behavioral Therapy

One model of therapy often associated with short-term treatment is **cognitive behavioral therapy (CBT)**, which involves efforts to change patterns of thinking.

A key concept in CBT is that of **core beliefs**. Core beliefs, generally formed early in life, are an individual's views about themselves, other people, and the world in general. Because of confirmation bias, individuals tend to take in evidence that aligns with these core beliefs but not evidence that would refute their core beliefs. Core beliefs typically exist outside of the individual's awareness.

Cognitive distortions are illogical and unhelpful beliefs. They may also be referred to as automatic or negative thoughts. Some examples of cognitive distortions include black and white thinking, jumping to conclusions, overgeneralization, magnification, minimization (also called mental filtering, which is ignoring or discounting the positives), personalization, catastrophizing, fortune telling, mind reading, emotional reasoning, "should" statements, labeling, and blaming.

Cognitive restructuring is a process of realizing the presence of cognitive distortions, identifying them through guided discovery, and reframing distortions into more rational and helpful beliefs.

Mindfulness and relaxation techniques are also used in cognitive behavioral therapy. These may include guided imagery, progressive muscle relaxation, or a body scan exercise.

Rational-Emotive Behavior Therapy

Rational-emotive behavior therapy (REBT), developed by Albert Ellis, is one of the earliest forms of cognitive behavioral therapy. Ellis theorized that emotional problems originated in a personal belief system that was not aligned with reality. REBT uses the ABC model, also known as the ABC(DE) model, to understand the interactions between thoughts, emotions, and behaviors. This is very similar to the concept underlying operant conditioning, in which an antecedent leads to a behavior, which in turn leads to a consequence.

In REBT's ABC(DE) model, difficult emotions are understood in the context of an activating event (A), irrational belief (B), and emotional consequence (C). REBT further helps the client to dispute (D) the irrational belief, leading to an effective belief (E).

Dialectical Behavior Therapy (DBT)

Dialectical behavior therapy (DBT), based on the work of Marsha Linehan, is an evidence-based treatment for borderline personality disorder and other problems of emotion dysregulation. DBT involves four components: individual therapy, group skills training, in-the-moment telephone skills coaching, and therapist participation in a consultation team. Individual DBT is focused on target behaviors to increase or decrease based on the client's treatment plan. Skills training and coaching focuses on four areas: mindfulness, interpersonal effectiveness, emotion regulation, and distress tolerance.

Behavioral Modification

Based on operant conditioning, **behavioral modification** involves the use of positive reinforcement and modeling along with, to a lesser extent, punishment for undesired behaviors.

Positive Psychology

Positive psychology focuses on ideas of optimism, resilience, hope, and motivation. In this way, it is consistent with the strengths perspective in social work. In this case, the social worker seeks to increase the client's sense of happiness and experience of well-being, focusing on increasing desired emotions and activities rather than focusing on the client's problems or symptoms.

Reminiscence Therapy and Life Review

In working with older adults, **reminiscence therapy** is a model for treating memory loss and the loss of cognitive abilities associated with dementia. Using the five senses, clinicians help clients to recall people, places, and events from different times in their lives.

Similarly, **life review** is a process of looking back over one's life, analyzing its themes and deriving meaning in one's life experiences. Social workers use a life review process with older adults to assist clients in developing a sense of meaning and in affirming meaningful aspects of their lives and identities.

Trauma-Informed Care

Trauma-informed care is described in several different theoretical models, but all include common components of establishing safety and stability, providing case management to meet basic needs, addressing issues of grief and mourning related to the traumatic event, and supporting reconnection and reintegration. Because any person can have a history of trauma, trauma-informed care requires treating every person with open-mindedness and compassion.

One concept to be aware of when working with survivors of intimate partner violence is **trauma bonding,** which describes the emotional attachment that forms between an abuser and a victim. Trauma bonds have been found to form in a wide range of exploitive relationships. Victims experience abuse, control, and dependency on the one hand, while also experiencing love, admiration, and gratitude for the abuser at the same time.

Use of The Miracle Question

The **miracle question** is a technique drawn from solution-focused therapy. In this technique, the social worker asks the client to imagine a possible world in which their problems no longer exist and their issues have been addressed. In its different forms, this question serves the purpose of leading the client to begin to develop insight and explore their goals for therapy.

Social Work Practice with Individuals Across Treatment Settings

Inpatient Settings

In an inpatient medical setting, social workers provide case management and discharge planning. In an inpatient psychiatric setting, on the other hand, social workers may also provide mental health assessments and psychotherapy.

Milieu Therapy

In an inpatient psychiatric setting, one component of treatment is the therapeutic treatment environment, which is referred to as milieu therapy.

Outpatient Settings

Social workers providing outpatient mental health services may work in an agency, school, clinic, or private practice setting. Outpatient services may consist of the traditional weekly therapy session, or may involve more intensive individual and/or group therapy.

Day Treatment

Individuals who require more intensive treatment for mental health and/or substance use problems sometimes receive day treatment, also called intensive outpatient treatment. Day treatment programs typically provide multiple sessions of individual and group therapy for 5 or more days per week.

Psychopharmacology

In direct practice treating clients with mental health disorders, social workers often collaborate with psychiatrists, psychiatric nurse practitioners, and primary care providers who prescribe psychiatric medication.

Here are some commonly prescribed psychiatric medications:

Fluoxetine (Prozac) is a selective-serotonin reuptake inhibitor (SSRI) that is commonly prescribed for depressive and anxiety disorders.

Sertraline (Zoloft) is also selective-serotonin reuptake inhibitor (SSRI) that is commonly prescribed for depressive and anxiety disorders.

Note: SSRIs, in particular, are known for causing sexual side effects such as lower libido, difficulty reaching orgasm, and difficulty obtaining or maintaining an erection.

Bupropion (Wellbutrin) is an antidepressant belonging to the category of norepinephrine and dopamine reuptake inhibitors (NDRIs). NDRIs are less likely than selective serotonin reuptake inhibitors (SSRIs) to cause sexual side effects.

Alprazolam (Xanax) is a benzodiazepine (tranquilizer) medication that is used to treat anxiety and panic disorders

Haloperidol (Haldol) is an antipsychotic medication used to treat schizophrenia.

Risperidone (Risperdal) is also is an antipsychotic medication and is used to treat schizophrenia and bipolar disorder.

Dextroamphetamine-amphetamine (Adderall) is a stimulant medication used to treat attention deficit/hyperactivity disorder.

Methylphenidate (Ritalin) is also a stimulant medication used to treat attention deficit/hyperactivity disorder.

Social Work Practice with Couples

Couples are considered a family subsystem. Couples therapy should not be provided when there is physical violence in the relationship. One reason for this is that therapy may bring conflicts to the surface and increase the risk of continued violence. Another reason for avoiding couples therapy in cases of physical violence is that it may be inappropriate to focus on the relationship system when only the abusive partner is responsible for this behavior.

When conducting couples therapy, it is especially important that social workers are attentive to issues of confidentiality. Unless disclosure is mandated due to imminent risk, child abuse or neglect, or a court order, social workers should not disclose information collected in couples therapy without the consent of both partners. In addition, social workers should discuss with clients how confidentiality will be handled if one partner shares information with the therapist outside of the couples' sessions.

Social Work Practice with Families

When working with families, social workers view the family system or sub-system (such as a couple or a parent-child dyad) as the client. The focus of treatment is on improving the functioning of that system in relation to its environment.

Child welfare systems exist to support family life, supplement the roles of family members, and, at times, to substitute for the role of the family in caring for children. Many children who encounter the child welfare system have experienced some form of trauma. Therefore, a trauma-informed care approach is especially important.

Family life education is a multidisciplinary, empowerment-focused, strengths-based model of psychoeducation that seeks to provide families with knowledge and skills to make decisions that support healthy family functioning. Families are taught to recognize and build on their strengths, as well as to draw on their strengths during difficult or stressful periods. Family life education is intended to empower families before crisis occurs so that families can utilize their strengths when needed. Family life education is based on primary and secondary prevention strategies.

In family therapy, it is common for families to "scapegoat" one member. In this scenario, a family may visit a social worker describing the problems with that one family member and asking that the social worker "fix" that person. The social worker's role is to redirect the focus to the family system and to the interactions between each family member and the family as a system.

Social Work Practice with Groups

Social workers work with task groups as well as psychotherapy groups. In clinical practice, social workers may lead groups focused on helping clients find support for a particular life experience, or to help clients recover from mental health or substance use problems. In macro practice, groups may be focused on advocacy or community organizing.

Groups may be **open groups**, meaning that group members may join at any time, or **closed groups**, in which all group members begin in the group at the same time.

Group therapy offers several advantages as a treatment modality. Groups give clients a sense of community as well as an understanding that they are not alone.

In groups, clients learn to find and give support as they interact with one another. Social workers should encourage clients to share their experiences and feelings with the group. When clients approach the social worker about issues they have not shared in the group, the social worker should support the client in bringing up these feelings at the next group session. This encourages the client to benefit from the support of the group as a system.

Of course, in certain instances the social worker should meet individually with a client who is part of a group. These circumstances include disclosure of child abuse or neglect (which must also be reported), concern about suicidal or homicidal ideation, and when a group member needs further referral (i.e., for substance abuse treatment).

However, group work does create risks to confidentiality. The social worker should discuss confidentiality expectations with the group, so that members know that they should not share information about group members outside of the group. However, social workers should inform clients as part of the consent process for group work that the social worker cannot guarantee that other group members will maintain confidentiality.

Two concepts that social workers should be aware of in groups are groupthink and group polarization.

Groupthink is a psychological phenomenon in which group decision-making produces an irrational or dysfunctional outcome as a result of group members' tendency to minimize conflict based on a desire for harmony and conformity. In cases of groupthink, team members do not feel comfortable expressing their doubts, and pursue a course of action based on the apparent group consensus without considering alternatives.

Group polarization, on the other hand, is the tendency for groups to shift toward extremes in decision making, and thus coming to decisions that are either more cautious or more risky than group members would have made on their own.

Group Development and Functioning

According to **Tuckman's theory of group development,** groups go through the stages of forming, storming, norming, performing, and adjourning. The social work role actually begins before the group's forming stage, as the social worker is involved in pre-group screening, planning, and organization.

Through the stages of group development, group members move from independence to dependence and interdependence, and then again back to independence.

The **forming** stage involves members becoming acquainted with the group structure and with one another. Group members in the forming stage typically avoid conflict, wishing to be accepted by the group, and look to the group facilitator for guidance and direction.

In the **storming** stage, group members begin to engage in group processes and tasks, which may lead to the surfacing of interpersonal conflicts. Group members may compete for control, and leaders may begin to emerge.

In the **norming** stage, the group develops a sense of cohesion and begins to share leadership among multiple members. Trust develops and the group is able to function as a unit.

The **performing** stage involves interdependence, as group members adapt to meet each others' needs. Not all groups reach this stage. However, for those that do, it is highly productive.

Finally, the group reaches the **adjourning** stage as its purpose is complete and members separate. The adjourning stage is also referred to as the mourning stage.

Social Work Practice at the Organizational Level

Social workers providing interventions at the organization level may be involved in administration, service planning, and program evaluation. **Administration** involves the bringing together of resources in order to achieve an organization's goals, while **service planning** utilizes results of a needs assessment to create programs to meet client and community needs. **Program evaluation** is a research process for determining the effectiveness of the services provided.

When working in an organization, a social worker is likely to encounter elements of **bureaucracy**. **Bureaucracy** is defined as the complexity of rules and regulations and the hierarchical structure within a government, administrative, or social system.

Various theories are used in management of organizations. One theory, **scientific management theory**, views the functioning of an organization in terms of productivity and efficiency and advocates the use of the scientific method in determining workplace practices.

Another theory is **human relations theory**, which prioritizes positive social bonds and improved working conditions in order to support employee motivation and productivity.

Human Resource Management

In a **human resource management** role, social workers should use a person-in-environment perspective in working with employees and should use best practices to promote organizational effectiveness and equity. The use of job descriptions is one way to ensure that employees know what is expected of them, as well as to reduce bias in the hiring process. Upon hiring a new employee, a social work administrator should review the job description with the employee and provide them with a copy of it.

Change Management

Change management is a process of continuing to revise and renew an organization's direction, structure, and capacities based on evolving needs of internal and external stakeholders. Stages of change management include problem identification, organizational analysis, proposal of a solution, and planning and managing change.

SWOT Analysis

SWOT analysis refers to an organizational study that seeks to identify the organization's strengths, weaknesses, opportunities, and threats. In conducting this analysis, an organization gains insight into issues that can be addressed through strategic planning. SWOT analysis is typically conducted by a strategic planning committee as a baseline assessment in order to understand the organization's internal resources and capacities, as well as outside forces that will affect the organization going forward. In addition, a SWOT analysis will identify factors critical to the success of the organization as well as the organization's distinctive competencies.

Social Work Practice with Communities

Community Needs Assessment

In the **community needs assessment** process, the social worker will identify assets and needs in the community that the social worker can help to mobilize for improvement and change. This will include an identification of the gaps in services that can be filled to meet the community's needs. After conducting the community needs assessment, the social worker should then establish a planning team or task force, define the goals and objectives of the program, develop an action plan, and implement that action plan.

Community interventions are focused on empowering communities to improve their members' wellbeing.

Interventions at the community level follow these steps:

- Engagement of the affected community
- Identification of the problem or need to address
- Mobilizing resources within the community to address the problem or need
- Identifying community strengths and solutions to problems
- Developing and implementing an action plan
- Evaluating the intervention and planning for follow-up

Whenever possible, it is preferable to intervene in a way that transforms social systems rather than simply help the individuals affected by injustice and inequity.

Community Organizing

Community organizing uses both conflict and consensus approaches, helping people to understand their shared problems and to work together toward solutions. Community organizing seeks to build on social connections to support collective action in a sustainable way. Community organizing can take various forms including social planning, social action, and social development.

Community education is an aspect of community organizing and development, and involves efforts to help the public understand a social problem. Community education can serve a range of functions, including advocacy and health promotion.

Social Action

Social action refers to collective efforts directed toward a shared goal, such as addressing macro level problems and conditions in a community or society.

Locality Development

Locality development involves community-driven efforts to improve the quality of community life for residents in a neighborhood, such as by developing programs and services and building community support systems.

Social Planning

Social planning is a term that describes the fact-finding process of determining the social problems that need to be addressed in the community and identifying possible solutions.

Advocacy

Social workers fulfill the role of **advocate** through their work at all systems levels. In individual and family work, advocacy involves efforts to access resources with and on behalf of clients in order to meet their needs.

In community advocacy work, social workers move from **case to cause** as they assess structural inequities that negatively impact clients and provide interventions designed to combat social injustice. Advocacy for clients is based on the social worker's understanding of clients in their environments.

Social workers should continue to support policies that help to address the needs of vulnerable and marginalized communities, as well as to address policy changes that make access to needed services and supports more difficult. Social services in the United States and several other countries have been impacted by **devolution**. Devolution is a process by which the responsibility for social welfare programs is shifted from the national (federal) government to state, provincial, or local governments. Devolution has resulted in significant changes to how social service programs are administered, and has caused the closing of small community-based organizations as local social service providers compete for limited resources.

Research and Evaluation

Following the intervention phase, it is important to evaluate progress. It would not make sense to terminate services without determining the extent to which goals have been met. If the client's goals have not yet been met, perhaps continued services are needed. On the other hand, if all goals have been reached, the social worker

Research is the creation and dissemination of knowledge. Social work research seeks to determine effective solutions to social problems, including the development of interventions, treatments, and policies. Even if you are not a researcher yourself, you are hopefully implementing interventions based on the results of research.

All social workers must have skills for carrying out and interpreting research. Research in social work should empower the clients and client systems who are most affected by its use.

Historically, research has not adequately served marginalized and oppressed groups such as women and people of color. Women and people of color have been excluded from many of the studies that have been used to develop our most well-known psychological and social theories. In addition, researchers have taken advantage of women and people of color, conducting experiments in ways that have caused harm and, in particular, harm to women and people of color.

Today, research activities involving human subjects must be reviewed by an **Institutional Review Board** (IRB, in the United States) or **Research Ethics Board** (REB, in Canada) to ensure the protection of participants.

Sampling Methods

There are a number of different sampling methods used in research including both **probability sampling** and **non-probability sampling** methods.

One type of non-probability sampling method is a **convenience sample**, which is a sample selected based on availability. Often, in social work research, it is impractical or cost-prohibitive to create a random sample from the entire population of interest. For this reason, convenience sampling is often used. Similarly, many psychological studies have been conducted using undergraduate college students as a convenience sample. With convenience sampling, there are potential limitations to the sample's representativeness of a larger population.

Sample Size

An important consideration in evaluating research is the **sample size** of a study. Studies with a large sample size produce results that are most likely to be generalizable to a larger population. A small sample size in a research study, on the other hand, limits the generalizability of the results to the larger population. The smaller the sample size, the lower the likelihood that the sample is representative of that larger population. As a result, there is a greater potential for the characteristics of the larger population to be different from those of the small sample that is studied.

Validity and Reliability

Validity refers to the extent to which a measure accurately measures what it is intended to measure.

Reliability refers to how consistently a measure will produce the same results each time. One type of reliability is **inter-rater reliability,** which describes the degree of agreement between multiple individuals who observe responses or phenomena and assign ratings or codes to their observations.

Note: A measurement tool may be reliable but not valid. However, it cannot be valid if it is not reliable.

Pretest-Posttest Designs

Pretest-posttest designs are used in both experimental and quasi-experimental research and involve taking measurements both before and after the intervention being studied. Pretest refers to preliminary measures administered in advance of an intervention in order to establish a baseline level. Posttest measures, on the other hand, are measurements administered after the study intervention, which collect data for comparison with the pretest results.

In such a design, the intervention type and/or extent of intervention provided at a particular point would represent the independent variable(s), and the results of the assessment measures would represent the dependent variable(s).

Independent and Dependent Variables

An **independent variable** is defined as a condition or quantity that is changed or controlled by the experimenter. A **dependent variable** in a research study is a condition or quantity that is studied based on a hypothesis that it will change based upon the independent variable. In other words, the dependent variable is being studied through a change or changes made to the independent variable.

Causal Fallacies

A **causal fallacy** is a logical error in which one concludes that an event that occurs first is the cause of an event that follows. There are several types of causal fallacies, the most common of which is the correlation/causation error.

Inductive and Deductive Reasoning

Inductive reasoning involves using observations and experiences to create new theories. Inductive reasoning is typically used in qualitative research methods, which favor observation and interviewing and seek to describe the complexity of people's experiences. Inductive reasoning can be contrasted with deductive reasoning (also called the hypothetico-deductive method), which begins with a hypothesis that is tested in order to support or falsify a theory.

Deductive reasoning, also referred to as hypothetical-deductive reasoning or the hypothetical-deductive method, is a "top-down" approach in which an individual begins with a hypothesis or theory, and then tests whether or not their observations fit with this hypothesis or theory. In this way, they can reason based on general principles in order to determine specific facts.

Grounded Theory

Grounded theory is an approach to qualitative research that begins with collecting observations and involves looking for patterns and themes that emerge from those observations. This involves the application of inductive reasoning rather than deductive reasoning.

Evidence-Based Practice

Evidence-based practice involves the use of research findings to inform practice decisions. Evidence-based practice is a process for integrating evidence with clinical expertise and values to select effective interventions to help clients. To utilize evidence-based practice, social workers consider the client's diagnosis and demographic information, and review professional literature about this diagnosis and population.

By applying research findings, the social worker makes use of empirically-tested knowledge in order to serve clients in ways that are most likely to be effective. The evidence-based practice process can be applied not only to interventions, but also to assessment methods, understandings of a problem's cause, cost-benefit analysis, and to questions regarding the potential harm of an intervention.

Program Evaluation

One method of research is **program evaluation**, which seeks to assess the quality and cost-effectiveness of services in an agency. Program evaluation is a necessary skill for all social workers, as even a social worker in a clinical role may need to complete a program evaluation for funding or regulatory reasons. Program evaluation helps social workers improve services and determine which services should be provided to clients. In this way, the results of program evaluations can be directly applied to practice.

Through program evaluation, social workers can find out whether a program is achieving its intended goals, or whether the program may be ineffective or even harmful. Some interventions conducted by social workers and other mental health professionals have indeed been found to be ineffective or harmful. Even programs that appear to be based on sound theories may not work in practice. Thus, it is crucial to regularly evaluate the effectiveness and outcomes of social work programs.

Professional Values, Ethics, and Relationships

Social Work Codes of Ethics

The exam requires that you are familiar with, and that you are able to apply, professional social work ethical standards in your work with clients. Social workers in the United States should be familiar with the *National Association of Social Workers Code of Ethics*, and social workers in Canada should be familiar with the *Canadian Association of Social Workers Code of Ethics*. State and provincial boards of social work have adopted these codes as the basis by which they evaluate professional conduct. Either one will prepare you for this section of the exam.

While these codes of ethics are an important resource, keep in mind that all social workers are held to ethical standards regardless of membership in NASW, CASW, or any other organization. Licensing boards use these ethical principles in the adjudication of disciplinary matters. Codes of ethics may also be utilized in legal disputes as they are a standard, accepted reference for understanding social workers' duties as well as standards of care.

Social Work Core Values

Perhaps you decided to become a social worker when you realized that the values of the profession matched your own. As a profession grounded in humanistic and altruistic philosophies, social work maintains as its core values the following: service, social justice, human dignity, the importance of human relationships, integrity, and competence.

These core values are included in the *NASW Code of Ethics*:

Service

Social work is about using your skills to help people. As an ethical principle, the primary goal for social workers is to help those in need and respond to social problems.

Social justice

This is about reducing inequalities such as discrimination and oppression, as well as addressing the systems that privilege some groups of people over others. Social workers support policies that provide equal economic opportunities for all people.

Human dignity

Social workers support diversity and advocate for marginalized and oppressed groups. The value of human dignity also supports a social worker's non-judgmental stance and use of unconditional positive regard in client-centered relationships.

Importance of human relationships

One of the most important aspects of social work practice is the helping relationship. Social workers also recognize the importance of human relationships more broadly, and use relationships as a vehicle for change. In strengthening relationships among people, social workers promote and enhance well being at all levels.

Integrity

Social workers must act honestly and behave in a trustworthy manner. Social workers should practice self-care in order to support their ability to practice ethically and responsibly.

Competence

Competence as a social work value goes beyond the ability to carry out specific procedures. Social workers must utilize cognitive, critical, and self-reflective abilities to perform in interpersonal, professional relationships. Further, social workers should only practice within their areas of competence, referring to other professionals when needed.

Key Concepts in Social Work Ethics

Responsibility to Clients

According to the *NASW Code of Ethics*, social workers' primary responsibility is to promote client well-being. Clients' interests are, in general, the primary focus. The *Code of Ethics* further states that social workers are not to take unfair advantage of a professional relationship nor to exploit others for their own interests. Social workers should not prioritize their own self-interest over the interests of the client.

Supporting Client Self-Determination

An important social work value is supporting the rights of clients to make their own choices in their lives. Except in cases of imminent danger to self or others, social workers should not make choices on behalf of clients that go against their wishes, nor attempt to influence client decision-making.

Confidentiality and Its Limits

In general, information that clients share with social workers is confidential. Social workers should take measures to ensure client privacy. However, social workers are required to break client confidentiality in certain circumstances related to client danger to self or others, child abuse or neglect, and elder abuse. Social workers should explain to clients their policies related to confidentiality and its limits.

Duty to Warn

The concept of "duty to warn" refers to a mental health professional's obligation to inform potential victims, as well as the appropriate authorities, when a client threatens to physically harm others. In the United States, the concept of duty to warn comes from case law, specifically *Tarasoff v. Regents of the University of California*. Similarly, in Canada, courts have found that the duty to warn others of imminent danger can outweigh professionals' responsibility to maintain client confidentiality.

Informed Consent

Informed consent is the process by which a client grants a social worker and/or agency permission to use specific interventions. Informed consent should be based on a full disclosure of all information the client will need in order to make this decision. An informed consent document should include the purpose of the proposed treatment, risks of the proposed treatment, and any alternatives to the proposed treatment. This allows clients to decide for themselves whether or not they would like to proceed.

In most cases, informed consent is necessary before providing social work services. When working with children, the social worker should obtain informed consent from the parent or guardian and verbal **assent** from the child.

Working with Mandated Clients

When working with court-mandated and other involuntary clients, social workers should pay attention to potential challenges in engagement as well as their dual roles and responsibilities in relation to the client and the court. With court mandated treatment there are particular limits to confidentiality as the social worker must report compliance or noncompliance, and possibly more detailed information, to the court. Social workers should discuss these issues openly with clients.

Professional Boundaries

Social workers should maintain appropriate professional boundaries in order to avoid harming clients and in order to avoid harming the public's trust in the social work profession.

Avoiding Dual Relationships

Dual relationships are defined as situations in which a social worker and client experience multiples in relation to one another. Dual relationships create the potential for ethical violations and harm to clients. At the same time, dual relationships may at times be unavoidable. Dual or multiple relationships occur when a social worker relates to clients in more than one role, which may be professional, social, and/or business. Dual relationships can create the potential for boundary crossing, and can pose ethical concerns. Because of this, dual or multiple relationships are at times unethical. According to the *NASW Code of Ethics*, social workers should not engage in dual or multiple relationships with current or former clients when they pose a risk of exploitation or harm. At the same time, dual or multiple relationships are at times unavoidable, and must be navigated with clear, appropriate, and culturally sensitive boundaries.

Social workers may encounter conflicts, or potential conflicts, between their professional roles and relationships and their social, religious, sexual, or business roles or relationships. These conflicts are not always unethical, but they do carry the potential for problematic or unethical boundary crossings and boundary violations. A social worker might join a neighborhood association or community board and find that a client is also involved. Or, a social worker who attends religious services may see clients there on a regular basis. These situations should be handled with care to prevent boundary violations or breaches of confidentiality.

Managing Boundary Crossings and Avoiding Boundary Violations

Boundary crossings are not inherently unethical, but they do pose the potential for harm. A boundary crossing involves bending, but not necessarily breaking, professional boundaries with a client.

One example of a boundary crossing would be attending a client's wedding or graduation. While the social worker has no obligation to attend, and can decline based on their own personal limits, attendance at a client's significant life event is generally permissible and ethical if handled with sensitive and appropriate boundaries. If a social worker does attend a client's life event, it should be at the request of the client and the therapist must be careful to maintain confidentiality of the social worker - client relationship. The social worker, of course, should consider the clinical implications of attending or not attending the event.

Boundary violations are exploitative, manipulative, deceptive, or coercive actions that are harmful to a client.

Social workers should never engage in sexual contact with current clients. Social workers should also not engage in sexual relationships with client's relatives if this is a risk of exploitation or harm to the client. (This would nearly always be the case, and so you should not do it!)

Similarly, social workers are not permitted to engage in sexual relationships with former clients, unless the social worker assumes the burden of demonstrating that the client was not intentionally or unintentionally coerced, exploited, or manipulated. Again, this would be difficult to demonstrate, so it is definitely best to avoid entering into this situation.

In addition, social workers should not provide services to a former sexual or romantic partner.

Self-Disclosure

An important aspect of the helping relationship is the social worker's professional use of self. However, the social worker's disclosure of information about themself and their life is a delicate issue that must be handled in a thoughtful manner. Self-disclosure should be used only for the benefit of the client, and careful attention must be paid to boundaries and to the clinical implications of the disclosure.

Social Media and Online Searches

Social workers' use of social media websites and applications creates the potential for boundary crossings. According to the *NASW Code of Ethics,* social workers should be aware of their personal affiliations and online presence, and how their involvement online may impact their ability to work effectively with particular clients.

According to the *NASW Code of Ethics,* social workers should not accept requests from clients on social networking sites, and should not engage in personal relationships with clients on social media. This is to prevent boundary confusion, dual relationships, and potential harm. Social workers should also be aware of information they post online, including on social media, and its potential impact on their ability to work with particular clients and client groups. However, social workers may use social media in professional ways without engaging in direct communication with clients.

In general, social workers should not conduct online searches about clients without their consent. Exceptions to this are in cases of imminent danger.

Ethical Dilemmas

An **ethical dilemma** involves a difficult choice between two or more courses of action. This choice presents itself when the social worker encounters a situation in which multiple ethical principles appear to require conflicting professional actions. Addressing ethical dilemmas begins with identifying the ethical principles at stake

Termination and Social Work Ethics

In an ideal scenario, clients would complete the intervention phase of treatment, and a review of progress in the evaluation phase would demonstrate that goals have been met. Following this, clients would work through the **termination phase** before ending the social worker - client relationship.

While this can and does happen, there are many other scenarios in which termination is more complex. Termination may occur because a client requires a different level of treatment, or due to reasons related to insurance or payment. Or, clients may choose to terminate even if goals have not been met.

When the social worker, rather than the client, initiates termination, there are many ethical issues to consider in order to avoid client abandonment. Social workers must assess for safety, only terminating if the client does not pose a danger to self or others. If a client is being referred to a different provider while there are safety concerns, the social worker should ensure that the client has initiated treatment with the new provider before terminating treatment with that client.

In cases of **termination due to non-payment**, there are specific ethical considerations. Social workers must first ensure that clients have been informed of their outstanding balance. This may take the form of a written invoice. The social worker must also discuss the implications of non-payment, so that the client is aware that services will be terminated if they do not make payment. In addition, the social worker must assess for safety, only terminating services if the client does not pose a danger to self or others.

A social worker should not terminate services in order to pursue a business relationship with a client. In addition, a social worker should not terminate services in order to pursue a social or sexual relationship with a client.

Follow-Up After Termination

In some cases, it is appropriate and helpful to **follow up** with clients following the termination of services. Depending on client need, it may be necessary to follow up with a client to ensure that they have connected with the ongoing care to which they were referred. It is also helpful in some cases to reach out to a former client in order to reassess the need for further services.

Supervision

The *NASW Code of Ethics* states that social workers should provide supervision only within their areas of knowledge and competence. In addition, social work supervisors must set clear, appropriate, and culturally sensitive boundaries. Social workers providing supervision or consultation should not engage in dual or multiple relationships that pose potential harm to the supervisee.

Supervisors and supervisees should be attentive to issues of parallel process. **Parallel process** describes the ways in which the social worker's relationship with their supervisor impacts the social worker's relationship with clients.

Transference and Countertransference

Social workers should use supervision to discuss issues of transference and countertransference. **Transference** refers to a client's feelings, based on other past or present relationships, that are transferred to the client's relationship with the social worker. **Countertransference** refers to a social worker or therapist's feelings, based on other past or present relationships, that are transferred to the social worker's relationship with a client.

Client Reluctance and Resistance

It is normal to encounter client reluctance as well as client resistance. The social worker should use understanding and empathy, as well as negotiation skills when appropriate, in order to engage clients and work through resistance. When facing client resistance, the use of supervision can also be helpful.

Language Interpretation

Social workers should use qualified **language interpreters**, and not client's family members or agency staff not trained in interpretation, when they do not speak or sign the client's requested language. The social worker should face the client, rather than the interpreter, and should speak and listen directly to the client.

Representing Oneself to Clients and to the Public

According to the *NASW Code of Ethics*, social workers should accurately represent their education and credentials to clients, agencies, and the public.

Working with Multidisciplinary Teams

When working with multidisciplinary teams, social workers have the opportunity to provide a psychosocial perspective to the team's work in helping mutual clients. Social workers should use teamwork skills to collaborate effectively with other professionals, considering team interactions as an aspect of mezzo-level social work practice.

Student Interns

It is important for student interns to inform clients of their student intern status. Student interns should also inform clients of when their field practicum will end, in order to prepare clients for termination, and should also inform clients of their supervision arrangement so that clients are aware of what information will be shared and with whom.

Impairment of Colleagues

According to the *NASW Code of Ethics*, social workers who become aware that a colleague is impaired due to substance abuse, mental health problems, or other personal problems should speak directly with that colleague when feasible in order to assist the colleague in addressing the issue. Only once this has been done, and if the colleague has not taken steps to address this impairment, should a social worker take action through other channels.

Continuing Education

Learning in social work, as in any field, is a lifelong endeavor. After completing their graduate education, social workers should pursue continuing education and training throughout their career. Many licensing boards will require continuing education hours, but social workers should seek out training opportunities and also review professional literature on a regular basis even if there is not a specific hour or credit requirement.

Preventing, Recognizing, and Managing Burnout

While it is best to prevent burnout altogether, it is also necessary to have skills for recognizing and managing burnout when it arises.

Best practices for addressing burnout include practicing self-care, engaging in mindfulness activities, and connecting with other professionals. Further, a multi-faceted approach is often needed in cases of burnout, and so the correct answer is all of the above. **Burnout** takes the forms of depletion or exhaustion, increased distancing mentally from one's professional role, negativity or cynicism toward one's work, and reduced effectiveness in a professional role. Addressing burnout requires both structural and individual changes. At the individual level, addressing burnout requires multiple, ongoing forms of self-care (i.e., a lifestyle rather than a vacation), including mindfulness, along with engagement with a community of colleagues.

Self-Care

It is well-established that social workers should prioritize self-care, but this is also easier said than done. **Self-care** is more than occasionally treating yourself to something nice or taking a break, but instead requires structural measures to manage the structural problems that can potentially lead to burnout. Best practices for self-care include plenty of rest, healthy boundaries, utilizing social support. It is important to have a self-care plan and follow it consistently.

Compassion Fatigue

Compassion fatigue includes both emotional and physical exhaustion that inhibits one's capacity to empathize and feel compassion for others. It is caused by exposure to traumatic material and may have a sudden, rapid onset. Its symptoms can mirror those of post traumatic stress disorder.

Social Worker Safety

Attending to **worker safety** is important for any agency. Best practices for attending to worker safety include conducting a thorough clinical risk assessment for each client, providing high quality safety training for workers, and convening an agency safety committee in order to oversee the implementation of safe workplace strategies.

Subpoenas

Receipt of a subpoena from an attorney is not an ethical reason to disclose client information without consent. A subpoena is not the same as a court order, and an attorney who is not a judge does not have the authority to compel the release of records. In response to a subpoena, a social worker should claim privilege and should not provide records unless a court order is issued.

Court Orders

A court order signed by a judge does compel the release of confidential information. Even so, the social worker should protect the client by attempting to limit the scope of records required, and should request that records remain under seal.

Mandated Reporting

Suspected Child Abuse or Neglect

Social workers are **mandated reporters** of **suspected child abuse or neglect**, and should file such reports with the state or local jurisdiction based on jurisdictional requirements. As a mandated reporter, the social worker is responsible for making a report anytime there is suspected abuse or neglect of a child. This does not require the social worker to investigate further, although that may at times also be appropriate depending on the setting and situational factors. While consulting with a supervisor may also at times be appropriate or necessary for the social worker's assessment or intervention process, making the report of child abuse comes first and is not contingent on any supervisory guidance.

Suspected Elder Abuse or Neglect

In many states, social workers are also legally mandated to report situations of suspected elder abuse. Social workers should be aware of **elder abuse**, its signs, and reporting requirements. Elder abuse can include physical abuse, emotional or psychological abuse, financial exploitation, and neglect. Elder abuse reporting goes through state and local adult protective services (APS) agencies, which investigate and assess cases of suspected mistreatment of older adults as well as other vulnerable adults including abuse, neglect, and financial exploitation.

Whenever possible, clients should be informed about reports being made by a social worker.

Getting Ready for the Practice Exam

While it is important to study social work content for this exam and know it well, there is also an extent to which test-taking techniques must be learned through experience. With that in mind, I am providing you with a full-length, 170-question practice exam designed to simulate your experience on test day.

In order to prepare for the focus and endurance that your test day will require, I recommend setting aside 4 hours and taking the complete practice exam in one sitting. Of course, take short breaks whenever you need to – without stopping the clock. Choose a quiet space and a time when you will not be interrupted. Once you have completed the exam, you can use separate study sessions on the days that follow to review the detailed explanations that are provided for each correct answer choice.

A Note on the 2023 Test Update

Before 2023, ASWB exam questions each had 4 answer choices (A, B, C, and D). Starting in January 2023, some test questions will have 3 answer choices (A, B, and C) while other questions will have 4 answer choices (A, B, C, and D). The practice exam in this book is updated for this 2023 format.

Use this new format to your advantage, and make sure not to leave any questions unanswered!

1. A social worker is working with a client who was recently diagnosed with a terminal illness. The social worker asks the client if he has a will, and encourages the client to include the therapist in his will since the social worker has played a significant role in his life. This action by the social worker is:

A. Ethical, because the social worker is an important person in the client's life
B. Unethical, because the social worker is prioritizing their own self-interest over the client's best interest
C. Ethical, because the client still has the choice of whether or not to take this action

2. In a clinical research study designed to evaluate the effects of psychotherapy on alcohol use, participants are asked to complete rating scales at intake, during treatment, and again at the conclusion of the treatment intervention. The use of rating scales before the start of the intervention would be considered the:

A. Posttest
B. Pretest
C. Focus group
D. Mixed methods design

3. A social worker receives a connection request from a former client on a professional networking site. The client recently started a new business, which had been a significant goal of his during his work with the social worker. The social worker should:

A. Accept the connection request to honor the former client's progress
B. Decline the connection request
C. Ask a supervisor how to handle the situation
D. Respond to the connection request with open-ended questions in order to ascertain the former client's intentions

4. When meeting with a social worker during an initial intake session, a client reports that he enjoys being "the life of the party" and feels very uncomfortable when others are not paying attention to him. He states he often feels under-appreciated and disregarded by others. The client's MOST likely DSM-5 diagnosis is:

A. Histrionic personality disorder
B. Schizoaffective disorder
C. Borderline personality disorder
D. Narcissistic personality disorder

5. A client meets with a social worker and, when asked about his alcohol use, states that he drinks 4 or 5 beers daily and that it is causing problems in his marriage. He states that his spouse has asked him to cut down, but that he disagrees with his spouse and does not think that his drinking is a problem. According to the transtheoretical model, the client is MOST LIKELY in which of the following stages?

A. Preparation
B. Contemplation
C. Maintenance
D. Pre-contemplation

6. A social worker is working with a client who begins to exhibit symptoms consistent with a diagnosis of schizophrenia. The social worker has no training in how to help clients with schizophrenia. What should the social worker do NEXT?

A. Ask a supervisor to assist the social worker in session
B. Read about evidence-based interventions for schizophrenia
C. Refer the client to a support group
D. Refer the client to a colleague with experience working with clients who have psychotic disorders

7. Which of the following is true regarding supervision in social work practice?

A. Supervision should focus primarily on administrative tasks.
B. Supervision is unnecessary except for student interns.
C. Supervision can assist the social worker in addressing issues of countertransference.
D. Supervision should be provided only by licensed clinical social workers.

8. In a hospital outpatient program, a social worker participates in a weekly staff meeting. During the meeting, a discussion is held about an important decision to be made by the staff. Some team members privately hold doubts but do not feel comfortable expressing them. Without considering alternatives, the staff decide on the course of action that appears to generate consensus. This process among the program staff can be best described as:

A. Confirmation bias
B. Group polarization
C. Groupthink

9. All of the following are true regarding dual relationships EXCEPT:

A. Dual relationships can create the potential for boundary crossings
B. Dual relationships should always be avoided
C. Dual relationships can pose ethical concerns
D. Dual relationships are at times unethical

10. A social worker at a drop-in center for LGBTQ homeless youth is tasked with establishing a new program to address the increasing number of youth who have been seeking services beyond the program's existing capacity. In order to best serve this community, the social worker should FIRST:

A. Establish a community advisory board
B. Conduct a needs assessment
C. Clarify the program goals
D. Train the staff in cultural competency

11. When a research study is conducted using a small sample size, this results in limitations to the:

A. Validity of the measurements
B. Generalizability of the results
C. Reliability of the measurements
D. Correlation coefficient

12. Which of the following is associated with the concrete operational stage of cognitive development?

A. Object permanence
B. Animism
C. Conservation
D. Egocentrism

13. A client invites a social worker to attend the client's high school graduation ceremony. The social worker should NEXT:

A. Explore the clinical implications of the social worker's attendance or non-attendance
B. Request a consultation with an ethics expert
C. Inform the client that this is not something that social workers do

14. A social worker conducts a study in which she seeks to explore the lived experiences of queer youth of color by conducting interviews, transcribing the interviews, and coding the transcripts to discover themes that emerge from the data. The social worker is MOST LIKELY using:

A. Single-case design
B. Deductive logic
C. Grounded theory
D. Mixed methods

15. A 35-year old male client meets with a social worker after being referred by a family member who is concerned about the client's cocaine use. The client reports using cocaine several nights per week while out with co-workers. He then stays up all night and sleeps late into the afternoon, often missing important meetings at work. The client states that he does not have a problem, as he believes that most men his age use cocaine and that he thinks his family members are just uptight about drug use. The client is MOST LIKELY using the defense mechanism of:

A. Projection
B. Projective identification
C. Reaction formation
D. Denial

16. A social work researcher is conducting a program evaluation at a community based organization that serves unhoused clients. In reviewing program data, the researcher notices that during weeks that the program distributed higher numbers of umbrellas to clients, there were more days that it rained. The researcher erroneously concludes that the distribution of umbrellas caused the higher number of rainy days. This belief is BEST described as a:

A. Hypothesis
B. Heuristic
C. Correlation coefficient
D. Causal fallacy

17. Which of the following should be included in an informed consent document?

A. Purpose of the proposed treatment
B. Risks of the proposed treatment
C. Alternatives to the proposed treatment
D. All of the above

18. Two fathers drop their child off at kindergarten. The child is initially upset when the fathers leave, but soon adjusts and engages with others in the classroom. When the fathers return at the end of the school day, the child appears happy to see them and runs right over to them. The child's behavior most closely matches which of the following attachment styles?

A. Secure attachment
B. Avoidant attachment
C. Disorganized attachment
D. Preoccupied attachment

19. After working during a period of numerous client crises and difficult interpersonal dynamics in his agency, a social worker begins to notice symptoms of burnout. To best address the symptoms of burnout, the social worker should:

A. Prioritize self-care
B. Engage in mindfulness activities
C. Connect with other professionals
D. All of the above

20. The concept of "duty to warn" refers to:

A. A social worker's status as a mandated reporter for cases of suspected child abuse or neglect
B. A responsibility to inform potential victims, as well as authorities, when a client threatens to inflict physical harm on others
C. A component of the institutional review board process for approving research on human subjects

21. In developing a treatment plan for a client, a social worker considers the client's diagnosis and demographic information, and reviews professional literature to determine which interventions have been proven effective for this diagnosis and in this client population. Based on their review of the literature, the social worker selects the intervention with the strongest empirical data demonstrating its effectiveness. The social worker is employing the principles of:

A. Dialectical behavior therapy
B. Evidence-based practice
C. Heuristics
D. Quantitative research design

22. Before leaving for school in the morning, a child asks his father to cut his sandwich diagonally into triangles rather than down the middle. The child explains that, this way, he will have more food as the triangles look bigger than the rectangle-shaped half sandwiches. According to Piaget's theory of cognitive development, the child has not yet developed:

A. Conservation
B. Object permanence
C. Sensorimotor skills
D. Pre-operational thought

23. When providing services to clients, social work student interns should do all of the following EXCEPT:

A. Inform clients that services are being provided by a student
B. Discuss the student's end date and the process for termination
C. Identify as social workers when introducing themselves to clients
D. Inform clients of the student's supervision arrangement and what information will be shared with supervisors

24. A child welfare social worker is assisting with the foster care placement of a 6-month-old infant. The infant has had inconsistent caregiving due to alcohol abuse problems in both biological parents. The infant is MOST LIKELY to require support in navigating which developmental stage?

A. Latency
B. Trust vs. mistrust
C. Formal operational
D. Autonomy vs. shame and doubt

25. In a city impacted by worsening problems of air pollution, data have shown that the residents most impacted by poor air quality are low-income residents and people of color. A social worker at a community-based organization supports residents in an area with a high percentage of low-income people and people of color to advocate for policy changes to reduce sources of air pollution affecting this area. The social worker is MOST LIKELY utilizing principles of:

A. Person-in-environment theory
B. Ecological systems theory
C. Environmental justice

26. To diagnose a client with major depressive disorder, the client's symptoms must have lasted for a period of at least:

A. 2 weeks
B. 1 year
C. 10 days
D. 48 hours

27. A client meets with a social worker for an initial assessment. A number of times over the past couple of years, the client has experienced periods of several weeks in which he felt depressed, slept most of the day, had little appetite, and felt hopeless. More recently, he had a period of 8 days in which he was irritable, stayed up throughout the night for several nights out of the week, incurred significant credit card debt, and engaged in unprotected sex with multiple partners. The client's MOST LIKELY diagnosis is:

A. Bipolar I disorder
B. Bipolar II disorder
C. Disruptive mood dysregulation disorder
D. Schizoaffective disorder

28. A social worker is meeting with a student who was recently diagnosed with a learning disability. The student is having difficulty in her classes, and has not received any services or support from the school. To BEST meet the needs of the student, the social worker should:

A. Assess the student's ways of coping with the learning disability
B. Administer psychometric testing to assess the student's disability
C. Advocate for the student to receive the services that she needs from the school
D. Contact the mandated reporter hotline to report educational neglect

29. A social worker is involved in advocacy efforts to address the needs of the local indigenous population. She meets with a tribal leader as well as a group of active tribal members in order to learn more about their needs and collaborate on a plan of action. The individuals with whom the social worker is meeting are considered:

A. Client systems
B. Collateral contacts
C. Stakeholders
D. Trainers

30. In the United States, a number of social welfare programs previously managed by the federal government have been transferred to state governments, which are given block grants to administer these programs. The federal government then provides some limited oversight regarding how assistance is given. This process is known as:

A. Liberalism
B. Devolution
C. Macro practice
D. Radicalism

31. A client meets with a social worker and states that they identify as pansexual. The client's identification as pansexual likely means that the client:

A. Experiences sexual attraction only in the context of a strong emotional connection
B. Is bisexual
C. Is sexually and/or romantically attracted to people of any sex or gender

32. A client meets with a social worker for an initial session and describes problems that she is having at her job. She reports being assigned numerous simple, repetitive tasks even as her male colleagues, who hold the same job title and have less experience, are given more complex and interesting assignments. She has also been passed over for promotions over the past two years, even as male colleagues with lower qualifications have been promoted. The client's experience MOST closely reflects:

A. Unemployment
B. Disparate treatment
C. Bureaucracy
D. Minority status

33. A client meets with a social worker and describes feeling highly stressed and at times experiencing a depressed mood. The client is able to engage in reality testing. According to psychoanalytic theory, the client's experience can be BEST understood as:

A. Psychosis
B. Borderline personality
C. Neurosis
D. Histrionic personality

34. An analysis of health outcomes in a city has shown that individuals' likelihood of experiencing diabetes and asthma differ greatly based on factors such as race, immigration status, household income, employment, and insurance coverage. In this context, these factors are known as:

A. Social determinants of health
B. Presenting problems
C. Provider bias
D. Biopsychosocial assessment

35. In a psychotherapy group, a social worker supports clients to find solutions to problems and obtain support from other group members who face similar situations. The social worker's actions are most reflective of the principles of:

A. Cognitive-behavioral therapy
B. Case management
C. Empowerment
D. Psychoanalysis

36. In a first session with a client, a social worker inquires about a client's experiences with oppression and privilege with relation to race, class, gender, ability, and sexual orientation. The social worker is MOST likely applying which of the following theories?

A. Psychoanalytic theory
B. Feminist theory
C. Strengths perspective
D. Intersectionality theory

37. A school social worker is assisting in the Individualized Education Program process for a student as part of a multidisciplinary team. The social worker's role on the team is MOST likely to involve:

A. Conducting psychometric assessments
B. Ensuring medication compliance
C. Providing a psychosocial perspective
D. Tracking academic progress

38. The use of deductive reasoning is associated with which stage of cognitive development?

A. Pre-operational stage
B. Formal operational stage
C. Concrete operational stage

39. A client in psychoanalytic psychotherapy describes wanting to satisfy every impulse at the moment he feels it. He states he feels he must seek pleasure at all costs, and that he cannot consider values or morality in his decisions. According to Freud's structural theory, the client's desires are most likely driven by the:

A. Id
B. Ego
C. Superego
D. Oedipus complex

40. A social worker in a family services agency meets with a client. The client describes wanting to become "the best possible version of myself," which he sees as becoming employed so that he will feel accomplished, and also wanting to develop longer-lasting and more meaningful friendships. The client recently lost his food assistance benefits as he had difficulty with the recertification paperwork. Since that time, he has been limiting himself to one small meal per day as he has no consistent source of income. Based on Maslow's hierarchy of needs, the social worker should FIRST assist the client with:

A. Becoming his highest self
B. Access to food
C. Feeling accomplished
D. Developing friendships

41. A client meets with a social worker and describes feeling badly about himself. He states that he feels like a failure, as he has made many mistakes in his life and has not accomplished what he thought he would accomplish by this point in his life. In utilizing the principles of client-centered therapy, the social worker is MOST likely to focus on:

A. Establishing specific goals and objectives for the client
B. Analyzing the client's earliest memories
C. Providing unconditional positive regard and accurate empathic understanding
D. Cognitive restructuring

42. Conversion therapy, a pseudoscientific model that claims to change the sexual orientation of individuals from gay to heterosexual, is considered to be harmful because:

A. It has been found to increase suicidal ideation and other negative mental health outcomes
B. All major mental health organizations consider the practice to be unethical
C. It has been made illegal in many U.S. states and municipalities, as well as in Canada
D. It is associated with political controversy

43. A client meets with a social worker for help with his depressed mood. In his interventions, the social worker seeks to increase the client's sense of happiness and subjective well-being. The focus is on increasing desired emotions and engagement rather than on targeting symptoms. The social worker is most likely applying the principles of:

A. Positive psychology
B. Cognitive behavioral therapy
C. Interpersonal psychotherapy
D. Psychoanalysis

44. A client in a mental health agency meets with a social worker for help managing his anxiety disorder. In utilizing a strengths-based perspective, the social worker should:

A. Target and treat specific symptoms
B. Focus on client deficits
C. Identify inner and outer resources to support resilience
D. Refer the client for medication management

45. A clinical social worker conducts play therapy with a 2 year old girl. The social worker supports the client in making decisions about play and follows the client's lead as she asserts her wishes. The social worker is MOST LIKELY assisting the client in navigating the psychosocial developmental stage of:

A. Industry vs. inferiority
B. Initiative vs. guilt
C. Autonomy vs. shame and doubt
D. Formal operational thinking

46. Even as individuals and communities are impacted by trauma in significant ways, people can and do "bounce back" from difficult experiences and adapt. This concept is BEST described as:

A. Person-in-environment
B. The strengths perspective
C. Resilience

47. A school social worker assists an elementary school teacher in developing a program to help improve a child's functioning in school. The child has had difficulty with staying on task during lessons, and has instead been speaking out of turn and distracting other students. The social worker consults with the teacher to set up a system of positive reinforcement and modeling in order to gradually shape the child's actions toward those that will work best in the classroom environment. This approach is known as:

A. Behavioral modification
B. Positive punishment
C. Classical conditioning
D. Dialectical behavior therapy

48. All of the following are types of community organization practices EXCEPT:

A. Social action
B. Locality development
C. Social planning
D. Biopsychosocial assessment

49. A social worker in a facility for adults with intellectual disabilities meets with a client for an initial session. In order to most effectively determine the client's needs, the social worker should FIRST:

A. Conduct a comprehensive biopsychosocial assessment
B. Consult with family caregivers for collateral information
C. Develop a treatment plan based on the client's goals
D. Provide cognitive behavioral therapy

50. Upon hiring a new employee, a social work administrator should:

A. Explore likely countertransferential issues
B. Review the job description with the employee and provide them with a copy of it
C. Conduct a comprehensive biopsychosocial assessment
D. Develop a social relationship with the employee

51. A 49-year old woman employed at a local corporation is referred to a social worker by her employee assistance program. The client describes feeling anxious whenever she has to speak in staff meetings at work. She states that she will often avoid meetings, and when she does attend meetings she notices her palms sweating and her heart racing. The social worker assists the client in identifying the specific activating events and irrational beliefs that lead to her anxiety symptoms. The social worker is applying techniques of:

A. Dialectical behavior therapy
B. Rational emotive behavior therapy
C. Blended case management
D. Psychodynamic psychotherapy

52. An adolescent client in a refugee resettlement program meets with a social worker for an initial session. The client describes finding it difficult to understand her sense of who she is both as a person from her Afghan culture as well as her new experience as an American living in the United States. She describes finding some social expectations in the United States to be surprising to her, as they are different from those of her culture in Afghanistan. According to psychosocial development theory, the client is navigating the conflict of:

A. Trust vs. mistrust
B. Generativity vs stagnation
C. Identity vs. role confusion
D. Intimacy vs. isolation

53. A social worker recently began working in an administrative role, which requires that they supervise staff and develop a system for evaluating employee performance. In this role, the social worker should NOT:

A. Engage in dual relationships with supervisees
B. Set culturally sensitive boundaries
C. Supervise only within their areas of knowledge and competence

54. A hospital social worker meets with a patient who is recovering from surgery. The patient tells the social worker that she was injured in a car accident and, as a result of her injuries, will have limited mobility for several months. The patient lives alone. Based on the steps of the helping process, what should the social worker do NEXT?

A. Conduct a comprehensive biopsychosocial-cultural-spiritual assessment
B. Refer the patient to a rehabilitation facility
C. Develop a plan to evaluate the patient's physical recovery
D. Utilize evidence-based interventions for coping with trauma

55. A hospital social worker observes that a colleague has been acting differently in recent weeks. The colleague has been drinking heavily at after-work happy hours and has been arriving late to morning staff meetings. The colleague has been away from her desk for long periods of time, and has not kept up with documentation requirements. To address this issue, the social worker should FIRST:

A. Report the colleague's impairment to the attending physician
B. Discuss the issue with the social work department supervisor
C. Inform the relevant professional licensing board
D. Discuss these concerns with the colleague directly

56. The idea that mental health disorders result from interactions between a predispositional vulnerability in combination with life stressors is explained by:

   A. The stress-diathesis model
   B. Social learning theory
   C. Classical conditioning
   D. Single-case design

57. A 25-year-old male client meets with a clinical social worker for an initial session. The client describes feeling like he must work out at the gym every day and build muscle, as he feels pressure to meet certain physical standards in order to fit in socially. He checks his appearance in the mirror many times each day and worries that small pigmentation marks on his face make him appear "flawed." The client's most likely DSM-5 diagnosis is:

   A. Anorexia nervosa
   B. Eating disorder, unspecified
   C. Body dysmorphic disorder
   D. Bulimia nervosa

58. A social work researcher is seeking to understand the lived experiences of African-American teenagers and the ways in which they are impacted by racism. In order to refine her research questions, the social worker interviews a sample of members of the impacted community and codes her interview notes based on themes. The researcher appears to be using which type of reasoning?

   A. Inductive
   B. Deductive
   C. Mixed methods
   D. Quantitative

59. In a mental status exam, a person's subjective experience of their own feeling state is referred to as their:

   A. Affect
   B. Mood
   C. Thought content
   D. Euthymia

60. Which of the following is true regarding confidentiality when conducting couples therapy?

A. Couples therapy poses no specific challenges regarding confidentiality, and so confidentiality issues should be handled the same as in individual therapy
B. Social workers should keep information confidential unless both partners consent to disclosure, or in cases in which confidentiality must be broken
C. Either partner alone can consent to disclosure of clinical information

61. A social worker is developing a new agency program and seeks to determine in which location the program should be focused, as well as the types of services that should be provided. To BEST answer these questions, the social worker should conduct a(n):

A. Randomized controlled trial
B. Single-case design study
C. Needs assessment
D. ABAB design study

62. A social worker meets with a client who was recently diagnosed with dementia. Based on the social worker's assessment as well as the recommendations of the client's other treating providers, the client requires placement in a long-term care facility. However, the client is uninsured and has limited financial resources. In order to help this client access the care that he needs, the social worker should FIRST:

A. Discuss the situation with family caregivers to see how much they can contribute
B. Refer the client to alternative outpatient services that will be covered by the client's insurance
C. Assess the client's eligibility for insurance coverage that will cover long-term care
D. Provide psychoeducation regarding the effects of dementia

63. A social worker in an Early Head Start program meets with the parents of a two-year old child. The child has recently been shouting "No!" when he is given instructions, and he often seeks to choose his own activities rather than doing what his parents tell him to do. According to Erikson's stages of psychosocial development, the infant is MOST likely navigating the crisis of:

A. Intimacy vs. isolation
B. The oral stage
C. Autonomy vs. shame and doubt
D. Industry vs. inferiority

64. A social worker meets with an incarcerated client in a prison setting for an initial assessment. Based on this assessment, the social worker diagnoses the client with a mental health disorder. The social worker should NEXT:

    A. Develop a plan in collaboration with the client that includes case management and mental health treatment services

    B. Monitor the client's progress

    C. Refer the client for medication management

    D. Obtain previous treatment records

65. A veteran who recently returned home from active duty meets with a social worker. The veteran states that she feels depressed and frequently experiences nightmares from her time in the military. She states, "I can't take it anymore and I want to find a way out of this." What should the social worker do NEXT?

    A. Share the client's story to advocate for improved services for veterans

    B. Conduct a suicide risk assessment

    C. Contact the veteran's family members for collateral information

    D. Refer the client for a psychiatric evaluation

66. A client at a shelter for survivors of intimate partner violence meets with a social worker. The client describes missing her partner and wishing to return to her relationship, despite the physical abuse that she experienced. The client's feelings are most likely a result of:

    A. Classical conditioning

    B. Trauma bonding

    C. Post-traumatic stress disorder

    D. Negative reinforcement

67. A couple meets with a social worker and states that they have been having difficulties with intimacy because one of the partners experiences pain during intercourse. To best help this couple, the social worker should:

    A. Refer the partner experiencing pain for a medical evaluation

    B. Utilize cognitive behavioral therapy techniques

    C. Refer the couple to a sex therapist

68. A clinical social worker meets with a female same-sex couple for relationship counseling. The couple is expecting their first child in a few months, and they are having difficulty navigating the reactions of co-workers and family members. They have been asked several times which partner is going to be "more the Mom" and which partner will "have the Dad role." These questions are examples of:

A. Intersectionality
B. Microaggressions
C. Gender dysphoria
D. Systems theory

69. All of the following are reasons to terminate services to a client EXCEPT:

A. The client has an unpaid balance, the consequences of non-payment have been discussed with the client, and the client does not pose a danger to self or others
B. The client has reached their goals and does not require further services
C. The client's insurance coverage has changed and the client is being referred to a practice that accepts the new insurance
D. The client and social worker wish to pursue a business relationship

70. A social worker meets with a client for an initial session. The client states that he has been feeling sad and nervous ever since he became unemployed two months ago. He feels badly about himself and has difficulty sleeping. He spends much of the day consumed by worry thoughts about his future if he does not find another job. He states that, before he lost his job, he had never had any depression, anxiety, or sleep problems. The client's most likely DSM-5 diagnosis is:

A. Generalized anxiety disorder
B. Acute stress disorder
C. Post-traumatic stress disorder
D. Adjustment disorder

71. One clinical advantage of short-term treatment as compared to long-term treatment is that:

A. A known termination date can motivate the client and social worker to mobilize their resources to reach goals
B. It is more effective than long-term treatment because it involves the use of evidence-based interventions
C. It is covered by insurance, while long-term treatment is not

72. A client in an addiction treatment program meets with a social worker for help managing her cravings for alcohol. According to a strengths-based perspective, the social worker can BEST meet this client's needs by:

A. Identifying the client's inner resources and helping the client use those resources
B. Taking a "tough love" approach to discourage the client from relapse
C. Using the moral model of addiction to focus on individual choices
D. Referring the client to Alcoholics Anonymous in order to access regular group meetings and peer support

73. A mental health agency provides home visits to clients who would have difficulty attending appointments at the agency office. In order to provide home visits while attending to worker safety, the agency should do all of the following EXCEPT:

A. Conduct a thorough clinical risk assessment for each client
B. Exclude clients with mental health disorders
C. Provide high quality safety trainings for workers
D. Convene an agency safety committee to oversee safe workplace strategies

74. A 45-year-old female client meets with a social worker for an initial session. The client describes difficulties she is experiencing in her family. She states that her husband typically drinks alcohol throughout the day while working from home. The client handles most of the child rearing responsibilities for her two daughters, ages 8 and 10. She finds herself confiding in her older daughter and relying on her emotionally, as she feels as though her husband is emotionally absent. The dynamic between the mother and her older daughter is BEST described as:

A. Enmeshment
B. Collateral contact
C. Symbiotic
D. Boundaried

75. In meeting with a client, a social worker uses his knowledge of a client and the client's history to attend to how the client is likely to experience his words and actions. The social worker adjusts his actions based on this knowledge and understanding. The social worker's behavior is MOST reflective of:

A. Social diagnosis
B. Anticipatory empathy
C. Case management
D. Unconditional positive regard

76. A client meets with a social worker 10 days after the client's wife passed away. Since her wife's death, the client has been feeling extremely sad and hopeless. She reports having little appetite, low energy, difficulty sleeping, and moving very slowly. According to the DSM-5, the client likely has which of the following at this time?

A. Major depressive disorder
B. Complicated grief
C. Uncomplicated bereavement

77. A caseworker at a local social service agency is referred to a social worker through his Employee Assistance Program. Based on the social worker's assessment, the caseworker requires a higher level of care than the social worker can provide in this agency setting. The social worker should NEXT:

A. Meet with the caseworker for the number of sessions to which he is entitled
B. Refer the caseworker for the services that he needs
C. Discuss the case with the caseworker's supervisor
D. Request an ethics consultation

78. A group of neighborhood residents meets to discuss problems with noise pollution in the area. A social worker employed by the neighborhood association assists the group in facilitating the process of advocating for themselves and pursuing change. The social worker is engaged in:

A. Social work research
B. Community organizing
C. Case management
D. Case-and-cause advocacy

79. In the life model of social work practice, the concept of habitat refers to:

A. Building houses for low-income families
B. Rural or urban environments including residences, workplaces, and public amenities
C. Stages of psychosocial development
D. Force field analysis

80. A client is having difficulties with speech and swallowing. Extensive medical tests have not shown any physiological cause for these symptoms. Based on the DSM-5, the patient's most likely diagnosis is:

A. Somatic symptom disorder
B. Conversion disorder
C. Histrionic personality disorder
D. Persistent depressive disorder

81. A client meets with a social worker and describes having recently been to many medical appointments. Recently, the client intentionally injured himself in order to receive medical care. He has also created false medical records in order to create the appearance of having chronic medical conditions. He has not applied for any disability benefits and states that he enjoys his job. What is the client's MOST LIKELY DSM-5 diagnosis?

A. Malingering
B. Factitious disorder
C. Conversion disorder
D. Dissociative amnesia

82. Which of the following is NOT an ethical reason to disclose client information without consent?

A. The social worker receives a subpoena from an attorney
B. The social worker receives a court order signed by a judge
C. The client is at imminent risk of suicide
D. The social worker suspects child abuse or neglect

83. In a research study, a social worker collects baseline data regarding each participant's anxiety and depressive symptoms. The social worker then provides each participant with 10 sessions of cognitive-behavioral therapy. Following the termination of treatment, the social worker requests that each client fill out a new set of questionnaires regarding their symptoms. The measurements taken following the conclusion of treatment are considered the:

A. Single subject design
B. Posttest
C. Construct validity
D. Independent variable

84. In work with organizations, the concept of a SWOT analysis refers to efforts to analyze which of the following factors?

A. Strengths, wishes, opportunities, and threats
B. Strengths, weaknesses, opportunities, and threats
C. Strengths, weaknesses, opportunities, and treatments
D. Social factors, weaknesses, opportunities, and triangulation

85. A client at a social services agency recently came to the United States from Afghanistan, which she fled due to persecution. Which of the following terms describes the client's MOST LIKELY status in the United States?

A. Asylum seeker
B. Economic migrant
C. Social class

86. Which of the following is TRUE regarding social workers' presence on social media websites and applications?

A. Social workers should never utilize social media
B. Social media use creates the potential for boundary crossings
C. Social media use is prohibited by the professional Code of Ethics
D. Social workers should use social media for personal, non-professional purposes only

87. A social worker at a substance abuse treatment facility provides outreach and education to the community when the agency opens a new methadone treatment program. In response to vocal opposition by a small group of neighborhood residents, the social worker provides information regarding the benefits of the program under development as well as its intended client population. The social worker is engaging in:

A. Community education
B. Research
C. Psychoeducation
D. Community needs assessment

88. A social worker is developing a research design plan and decides to recruit clients from the agency where he works as his sample, in order to avoid the difficulty and expense that would be involved in sampling from the larger population. This method of sampling is known as:

A. Random
B. Purposive
C. Convenience
D. Mixed methods

89. All of the following are stages involved in change management EXCEPT:

A. Problem identification
B. Organizational analysis
C. Parallel process

90. A social worker is conducting a research study in which he seeks to determine the impact of providing motivational interviewing to clients who are court mandated to receive counseling services. This intervention will be compared to treatment as usual in order to determine whether or not it reduces recidivism rates. In this study, recidivism rates are considered the:

A. Independent variable
B. Dependent variable
C. Control
D. Experimental research design

91. A social worker has an account on a mobile dating application and receives a message from a former client. The former client asks the social worker if she would like to meet for coffee. The social worker should NEXT:

A. Consult an ethics expert to find out how best to handle the situation
B. Explain to the former client that the social worker is actually no longer single
C. Meet for coffee with the former client
D. Decline the former client's invitation

92. An individual's mastery of Erikson's stage of integrity vs. despair is most associated with:

A. Hope
B. Wisdom
C. Competence
D. Will

93. A mental health agency conducts a research study in which participants answer open-ended questions in a written survey regarding their experiences of recovery from mental health disorders. In analyzing the data, trained social work clinicians score the written responses according to several qualitative metrics. To ensure that each social worker is scoring the responses in an equivalent manner, a sample of responses are checked by a second clinician. The issue being assessed by this quality control measure is:

A. Inter-rater reliability
B. Test-retest reliability
C. Content validity
D. Construct validity

94. A social worker in macro practice utilizes principles of critical race theory and develops practical applications of this theory in his community organizing interventions. This uniting of theory and action is known as:

A. Critical theory
B. Praxis
C. Pedagogy
D. Practice

95. In statistical measures of central tendency, the concept of the mean is BEST defined as the:

A. Middle
B. Extreme
C. Outlier
D. Average

96. A 45-year-old woman meets with a social worker. The client describes feeling overwhelmed and exhausted ever since she became involved in arranging for her elderly father's care needs last year. She has had difficulty taking care of her own physical and emotional health during this time. The client is MOST LIKELY experiencing:

A. Major depressive disorder
B. Caregiver stress
C. Generalized anxiety disorder
D. Complicated grief

97. Which of the following is true regarding professional codes of ethics?

A. They provide a list of all ethical dilemmas a social worker may encounter
B. They provide step-by-step instructions for how to handle each ethical dilemma
C. They include core values and ethical principles
D. They contain recommendations but not requirements

98. An adolescent client meets with a social worker and describes feeling devastated by her awareness of climate change and the likelihood of increased natural disasters occurring as a result. To best assist this client, the social worker should FIRST:

A. Validate the client's feelings
B. Review ecological theories
C. Obtain continuing education in green social work
D. Utilize the person-in-environment perspective

99. A social worker meets with an elderly client in a long-term care facility and works with the client to complete a life review. The client describes struggling to see a sense of meaning in his life, feeling that he has not sufficiently given back to others and to the larger society. The client is likely having difficulty with which psychosocial crisis?

A. Autonomy vs. Shame and doubt
B. Integrity vs. Despair
C. Industry vs. Inferiority
D. Self-actualization

100. All of the following are true regarding social work ethics EXCEPT:

A. Social workers are prohibited from having sexual relationships with current clients
B. Dual relationships should be avoided when possible
C. Client self-determination is always the social worker's main priority

101. A child has been getting up from his seat during class, which has resulted in disruption to other students' learning. In an attempt to eliminate this behavior, the teacher takes away 5 minutes of recess time for each time the child gets up from his seat. The child, however, is relieved about losing recess time as he feels inadequate in his athletic abilities. As a result, the child gets up from his seat more often during class. The teacher's action of taking away recess time represents:

A. Negative punishment
B. Positive punishment
C. Positive reinforcement
D. Negative reinforcement

102. During a heat wave, neighborhoods with a high proportion of low-income residents experienced temperatures several degrees higher than neighborhoods with a high proportion of wealthy residents within the same city. This difference has been attributed to a greater number of trees per square mile in the higher income areas than in the lower income areas. As a result of the higher temperatures, the low-income residents are more likely to face heat-related health emergencies. The impact of this disparity demonstrates aspects of all of the following concepts EXCEPT:

A. Social determinants of health
B. Structural inequality
C. Behavioral theory
D. Systems theory

103. A client meets with a social worker and describes an incident in his workplace that has been bothering him. The client identifies as a gay male and plans, with his partner, to pursue parenthood through surrogacy. The client shared his plans with a co-worker, who stated "You'll be a great mom – I can see you really have those maternal instincts even though you're a guy." The co-worker's comment is an example of:

A. Ecological systems theory
B. Gender equity
C. Diversity, equity, and inclusion
D. A microaggression

104. A White social worker employed by a Native American tribal health center finds that he is often offending clients as he does not understand cultural norms in the community in which he is working. What should the social worker do NEXT?

A. Request an ethics consultation
B. Seek cultural competency training and education relevant to the population he is working with
C. Ask clients to educate him about Native American culture so he can better understand cultural norms and values
D. Attend a Native American cultural event to immerse himself in the community

105. In conducting a research study, a social worker uses inductive reasoning, applying grounded theory in order to discover new theories as themes emerge from the data collected. Which approach is the social work researcher MOST LIKELY using?

A. Qualitative
B. Quantitative
C. Mixed methods
D. Single-case design

106. A client with alcohol use disorder is prescribed Antabuse (disulfiram), which causes him to have significant unpleasant effects any time he drinks alcohol. Because of these effects, he no longer associates alcohol with pleasurable feelings. From a behavioral perspective, the introduction of Antabuse represents a(n):

A. Conditioned stimulus
B. Unconditioned response
C. Aversive stimulus
D. Conditioned response

107. A researcher studying workplace culture in an organization finds that, up to a point, employees who are assigned more tasks are more productive than employees who are assigned fewer tasks. However, after a particular threshold, employees assigned the greatest number of tasks are less productive than those assigned a moderate number of tasks. Which of the following best describes the research findings?

A. Positive correlation
B. Causal fallacy
C. Negative correlation
D. Curvilinear relationship

108. A 75 year old client meets with a social worker at a skilled nursing facility. Based on the client's report, the social worker suspects that the client is being physically abused by facility staff. The social worker should NEXT:

A. Conduct a comprehensive biopsychosocial-cultural-spiritual assessment
B. Report the suspected abuse to the local adult protective services agency
C. Consult a supervisor for further guidance
D. Report the suspected abuse to the facility director or his/her designee

109. When working with clients who have experienced trauma, social workers should do all of the following EXCEPT:

A. Establish safety and stability
B. Provide case management to meet basic needs
C. Address issues of grief and mourning
D. Early initiation of imaginal exposure

110. A client tells a social worker about cultural experiences in the client's life with which the social worker is not familiar. To best help this client, the social worker should use which of the following stances?

A. Cultural expertise
B. Cultural humility
C. Cultural brokering

111. Which of the following medications is a selective serotonin reuptake inhibitor?

A. Lithium
B. Risperidone
C. Fluoxetine
D. Venlafaxine

112. A funding agency representative meets with a social work administrator regarding grant-funded services that the administrator oversees. The funding agency requests that the social worker gather data to demonstrate the effectiveness of the funded services. The social worker is MOST LIKELY to utilize which of the following methods?

A. Practice evaluation
B. Program evaluation
C. Single-case design
D. Randomized controlled trial

113. A heterosexual, married couple meets with a social worker after finding out that the husband is a carrier for cystic fibrosis. The husband describes feeling devastated by this news and guilty about the impact he believes it will have on his wife, as the two of them wish to become parents. What should the social worker do FIRST?

A. Review the genetic testing report
B. Assess the husband's knowledge of genetics
C. Acknowledge the husband's feelings
D. Ask the wife is she is impacted in the way her husband thinks she will be

114. A social worker performs a community needs assessment and develops a program to address the psychosocial challenges faced by senior citizens who attend a local senior center. At which system level is the social worker practicing?

A. Micro
B. Mezzo
C. Holon
D. Macro

115. A social worker is hired by a prison system to conduct mental health assessments of incarcerated individuals. Soon after beginning her new position, the social worker is asked by her supervisor to backdate psychosocial assessments and create documentation of services that have not been provided. What should the social worker do FIRST?

A. Provide the documentation requested by the supervisor
B. Discuss with the supervisor the social worker's concerns regarding unethical conduct
C. Contact the prison system's compliance department
D. Ignore the supervisor's request

116. A client is referred to a social worker by his psychiatrist after having recently been diagnosed with bipolar disorder. The client states that he does not understand the diagnosis and does not understand what the diagnosis means. The social worker explains the diagnosis to the client, including common symptoms as well as treatment options. The social worker's intervention is BEST described as:

A. Psychoeducation
B. Medication management
C. Wellness self-management
D. Behavioral therapy

117. A patient at a veterans' health care facility meets with a social worker. The patient begins the meeting by stating that he is extremely frustrated with the facility and that he is angry about having to wait so long for appointments. What should the social worker do FIRST?

A. Assist the client in filing an official complaint
B. Encourage the client to advocate for systemic change
C. Acknowledge the client's experience and feelings
D. Educate the client regarding agency policies

118. Alprazolam is a medication used to treat which of the following conditions?

A. Schizophrenia
B. Anxiety
C. Depression
D. Attention-deficit/hyperactivity disorder

119. A parent meets with a social worker and expresses concern that their 2-year-old child has been refusing to go to daycare. The child states that she does not want to go as she wants to stay home with the parent. Which of the following is the MOST LIKELY explanation for this behavior?

A. Regression
B. Separation anxiety disorder
C. Normal separation anxiety
D. Sublimation

120. A teacher refers a 9 year old student to the school social worker after the boy has been bullying other students. The student tells the social worker that he has been angry lately because his father has been yelling at him and threatening him physically. Which of the following defense mechanisms does the student appear to be using?

A. Sublimation
B. Displacement
C. Projection

121. A client meets with a social worker for an initial session. The client states he has difficulty maintaining relationships, as his emotions are "so up and down." He states that he often "burns out" the people in his life, and that he is afraid of being abandoned and alone. Which of the following is the client's MOST LIKELY DSM-5 diagnosis?

A. Major depressive disorder
B. Alcohol abuse
C. Borderline personality disorder
D. Schizoaffective disorder

122. Social workers accepting bartering as payment for services rendered is:

A. Always unethical
B. Ethical in rural communities only
C. Ethical in very limited circumstances

123. Which of the following is NOT a symptom of antisocial personality disorder?

A. Engagement in criminal behavior
B. Irritability and aggression
C. Lack of interest in social activities
D. Lack of remorse for one's actions

124. In a first meeting with a social worker, a client describes her sister as "the worst person ever." Later in the session the client describes her best friend, who she just met 2 weeks ago, as "the most wonderful friend in the world." The client describes having few long-term friendships and says that she often feels empty, which she tries to cope with through self-harm. Which of the following is the client's MOST LIKELY DSM-5 diagnosis?

A. Narcissistic personality disorder
B. Schizoaffective disorder
C. Major depressive disorder
D. Borderline personality disorder

125. A school social worker meets with a student who was referred by their teacher because the student has not been paying attention in class and has not completed assignments. The social worker believes that the student may have a learning disability. What should the social worker do NEXT?

A. Conduct psychometric testing
B. Develop an Individualized Education Plan
C. Refer the student for psychological testing
D. Provide cognitive-behavioral therapy

126. A recently married heterosexual couple meets with a social worker for relationship counseling. The husband states that he would have preferred to meet with the doctoral-level psychologist at the clinic, and proceeds to challenge the social worker's qualifications. The wife describes her husband as not showing empathy and never apologizing when he says something hurtful. She also states that her husband frequently exaggerates his achievements and abilities. The husband is MOST LIKELY to carry which of the following DSM-5 diagnoses?

A. Histrionic personality disorder
B. Social anxiety disorder
C. Schizoaffective disorder
D. Narcissistic personality disorder

127. A social worker in a prison setting meets with a 48-year-old man recently convicted of a multimillion dollar fraud scheme. The client states that he began stealing money from his parents and from friends when he was 14 years old. Around that time, he also abused animals on several occasions. Now, as an adult, his deceitful behavior has become more complex. The client states that he does not regret his actions but instead only regrets getting caught. The client appears to have which of the following DSM-5 diagnoses?

   A. Oppositional defiant disorder
   B. Antisocial personality disorder
   C. Conduct disorder

128. In an inpatient psychiatric unit, a hospital social worker meets with a patient who was brought to the hospital after a suicide attempt and, while on the unit, was diagnosed with borderline personality disorder. In planning for discharge, the social worker is MOST LIKELY to refer the client for:

   A. Solution-focused brief therapy
   B. Dialectical behavior therapy
   C. Intensive case management
   D. Co-dependents Anonymous

129. A social worker employed in a child welfare agency meets with a family that is having difficulty paying for basic expenses. They have been served with an eviction notice and recently could not afford to purchase groceries. The parents state they feel badly about not being able to adequately feed their 3 children, and that they have been more irritable toward each other recently. What should the social worker do NEXT?

   A. Obtain donated toys and books for the children
   B. Assess the family's eligibility for food and housing assistance
   C. Refer the parents for couples' counseling

130. Which of the following is the primary reason for documentation in a client's chart in a hospital setting?

   A. Continuity of care
   B. Risk management
   C. Legal requirements

131. A social worker at a community health center supervises a social work student intern. One day, when the intern returns from lunch, the social worker notices that the student smells of alcohol. Agency and school policies, as well as the state's social work regulations, do not allow the practice of social work while under the influence of alcohol. The student does not appear intoxicated, however, and is behaving normally. What should the social worker do NEXT?

A. Ignore the issue as the student is of legal drinking age
B. Speak with the student and have them go home for the rest of the day
C. Report the behavior to the agency security officer
D. Report the behavior to the student's school

132. A social worker is employed as an executive director at a community mental health agency. Several staff members approach the social worker regarding what they have determined to be a culture of racism within the agency. Staff report experiencing frequent microaggressions, and have noticed that employees of color are rarely promoted. What should the social worker do FIRST?

A. Organize a cultural competency training
B. Gather more details about the nature of the complaints
C. Acknowledge the complaints and thank the staff members for sharing their experiences

133. In a research study, a measurement tool is used by multiple observers and consistently generates the same or similar results regardless of the person making the observations. This finding indicates support for which of the following with regard to this measurement tool?

A. Construct validity
B. Generalizability
C. Internal consistency
D. Inter-rater reliability

134. A social worker is conducting a home visit as part of an Assertive Community Treatment program. During the home visit, the social worker speaks with the client's family members and obtains information regarding the client's recent functioning. This is an example of:

A. Macro practice
B. Collateral contact
C. Client empowerment
D. Treatment planning

135. At a First Nations community health center, a White social worker is employed in an administrative role. While working in this role, the social worker should do all of the following EXCEPT:

A. Involve First Nations people in service planning and provision
B. Seek out cultural competency training
C. Position the social worker as a cultural expert
D. Acknowledge the social worker's White privilege

136. A client who has been engaging in problem drinking meets with a social worker. The client states that she is noticing the negative consequences of her drinking, and thinks she should probably cut down or stop. However, she thinks this would be difficult, as everyone in her social circles drinks, and so she is not sure how or when she will be able to stop or reduce her drinking. The client thinks she can probably start drinking less within the next few months. Based on the transtheoretical model, the client appears to be in the following stage of change:

A. Pre-contemplation
B. Contemplation
C. Preparation
D. Relapse

137. An occupational health social worker facilitates a support group for injured workers with long-term repetitive strain injuries. The social worker provides psychoeducation about pain management and the clients support one another as they work on improving their quality of life. This group is an example of:

A. Primary prevention
B. Secondary prevention
C. Tertiary prevention

138. A social worker is providing cognitive behavioral therapy to a young child with obsessive compulsive disorder. The child has attended 2 sessions so far. The parents contact the social worker after the second session and express that they do not believe the child is making enough progress in therapy. The parents request that the child be transferred to a different social worker. What should the social worker do FIRST?

A. Educate the parents about obsessive compulsive disorder and the cognitive behavioral therapy process
B. Assign the client more homework in between sessions
C. Refer the client to a social worker with psychodynamic training

139. A researcher calculates the extent to which, in general, the values in the data set deviate from the mean. The researcher's calculation would be considered the:

A. Standard deviation
B. Range
C. Central tendency

140. With regard to accepting payment for services, social workers should, in general, do all of the following EXCEPT:

A. Take into account the client's ability to pay
B. Accept payment in the form of goods or services
C. Explain their policies regarding payment and how non-payment will be handled
D. Accurately bill for services provided

141. A high school student meets with a school social worker and shares that his family is experiencing housing instability and difficulty affording food. Based on systems theory, the social worker can expect that:

A. The student's family will be evicted
B. The family's food insecurity may last for a significant period of time
C. Family stressors will impact the student's performance at school
D. The housing instability will be resolved more quickly than the food insecurity

142. A social worker in a substance use disorder treatment program meets with a client who uses heroin. The client does not wish to stop use entirely, but wishes to minimize the risk of infectious disease as well as the risk of overdose. The social worker takes the approach of meeting the client where the client is and respecting client self-determination, and assists the client in locating needle-exchange programs as well as education about preventing overdose. This approach is BEST described as:

A. Abstinence
B. Harm reduction
C. SBIRT
D. Twelve-step

143. A research study seeks to collect information regarding the lived experiences of LGBTQ foster youth. Noticing that there has not been sufficient research regarding this population, the researcher seeks to identify themes and develop theories about the needs and experiences of LGBTQ youth in foster care, creating a background for further study. The researcher develops an unstructured study using open-ended interviews. This type of study is considered to be:

A. Exploratory
B. Explanatory
C. Descriptive

144. In an initial session with a social worker, a client who identifies as non-binary becomes tearful while describing experiences of gender discrimination in their workplace. They describe feeling angry and hurt. What should the social worker do FIRST?

A. Assist the client in filing a formal complaint
B. Ask the client how long they have identified as non-binary
C. Validate the client's feelings
D. Explore the client's earliest experiences of discrimination

145. An 8-year-old boy is referred to a social worker by his family physician because the client is having difficulties with communication and social interaction. In meeting with the client, the social worker notices him engaging in repetitive movements. The client's parents note that the boy does not engage with other children at school, instead keeping to himself. At home, he is highly focused on his model train set and spends several hours with it each day. The parents also tell the social worker that their son follows routines very closely and is sensitive to any change in his environment. The client's MOST LIKELY diagnosis is:

A. Intellectual developmental disorder
B. Autism spectrum disorder
C. Specific learning disorder

146. A court-mandated client meets with a social worker for an initial session. The client tells the social worker that she will not be sharing any information, as she did not choose to be there. The social worker should NEXT:

A. Remind the client of the treatment goals
B. Acknowledge the client's lack of choice regarding treatment
C. Assure the client of absolute confidentiality
D. Explain the voluntary nature of social work services

147. A client is having difficulty with the fact that she was recently diagnosed with borderline personality disorder. She tells her social worker that she finds a diagnosis of a personality disorder to be invalidating, and that she worries about what this condition will mean for her future. What should the social worker do FIRST?

    A. Share information about the social worker's own mental health journey
    B. Explore the client's feelings regarding the diagnosis
    C. Provide psychoeducation regarding borderline personality disorder

148. A 20-year old client who identifies as neurodivergent meets with a social worker. The client describes the ways in which she pays very close attention to detail. She has noticed that she does not generalize objects into groups, but instead categorizes each one individually. Using a strengths perspective, the social worker should NEXT:

    A. Discuss the importance of person-environment fit
    B. Provide psychoeducation regarding autism spectrum disorder
    C. Explore the ways in which the client has unique talents and opportunities

149. A 25-year-old male client has recently realized that he is gay. After hearing homophobic statements in his family throughout his life, he has come to believe these negative ideas about himself. Which of the following BEST explains this client's experience with negative beliefs about gay people?

    A. Asceticism
    B. Identification
    C. Sublimation
    D. Internalization

150. A school social worker meets with a high school senior who has recently begun dating. The student states he is not interested in his classes anymore because he is entirely focused on trying to be in a relationship. According to Freud's theory of psychosexual development, the student is in which of the following stages?

    A. Latency
    B. Phallic
    C. Oral
    D. Genital

151. A client was born in 1990 and is considered a millennial. According to the life course perspective, this is an indication of the client's:

A. Trajectory
B. Cohort
C. Turning point
D. Ecology

152. A father of a young child considers the likely thoughts and emotions of the child, using language and behaviors in a way that is responsive to the child's emotions and physical needs. The father's behavior is MOST reflective of:

A. Empathic failure
B. Attunement
C. Resilience
D. Authoritative parenting

153. A husband and wife, who are both cisgender, meet with a social worker after learning that they are both carriers for a hereditary disease. Neither of them has had any symptoms, and they do not know of anyone in their families having symptoms of this disease. The condition MOST LIKELY follows which of the following inheritance patterns?

A. Autosomal dominant
B. Autosomal recessive
C. Y-linked
D. Co-dominant

154. A family meets with a social worker for help with problems in communication. Each family member tells the social worker about their interactions with other family members and the ways in which they experience frustration and anger toward each other. Using a narrative therapy approach, the social worker is likely to focus on:

A. Improving family members' coping skills for when they feel angry or frustrated
B. Psychoeducation regarding styles of communication
C. The family's stories about how they experience their interactions with each other

155. A hospital social worker meets with the family of a patient who is undergoing cancer treatment. During the meeting, the social worker notices large bruises on one of the child's ears. When asked about the bruises, the father states that he lost his temper and hit the child. He describes having a very short temper ever since his wife's cancer diagnosis. What should the social worker do NEXT?

    A. Provide psychoeducation regarding Kubler-Ross' stages of grief
    B. Report the incident to the child protective services agency
    C. Continue to monitor the situation
    D. Contact a supervisor for further guidance

156. A 65-year-old client who was assigned male at birth meets with a social worker at a community health center. The client shares with the social worker that the client has realized that she identifies as female and wishes to be referred to using female pronouns. The client describes having had some awareness of her female gender throughout her life, but has only recently found the words to describe her experience. What should the social worker do FIRST?

    A. Refer the client to an agency that specializes in serving the LGBTQ+ community
    B. Thank the client for sharing this with the social worker
    C. Ask the client about her plans for physical transition

157. A 10-year-old client with an intellectual disability meets with a school social worker. The client describes feeling inadequate as he has difficulty completing academic assignments and is unable to keep up with what is happening in class. The social worker's interventions are likely to focus on the psychosocial developmental stage of:

    A. Autonomy vs. shame and doubt
    B. Industry vs. inferiority
    C. Generativity vs. stagnation

158. A 21-year-old male is referred to a college counseling center by his academic advisor because he has been sleeping throughout the day and missing most of his classes. Upon meeting with the intake social worker, the client states that he needs help because he is tired all the time and does not feel motivated to do anything. Through a comprehensive evaluation, the social worker finds that the client meets criteria for major depressive disorder. The client's experience of fatigue and amotivation is the client's:

A. Diagnosis
B. Presenting problem
C. Reason for referral
D. Treatment plan

159. A social worker at a crisis response program meets with a client who is feeling highly anxious. The client states that she was recently evicted from her apartment and is not sure what to do next. The social worker should FIRST:

A. Refer the client for shelter services
B. Help the client develop coping strategies
C. Conduct a biopsychosocial assessment

160. A client experiences severe discomfort when he is in crowded and enclosed spaces. When traveling on trains during rush hour, he experiences heart palpitations, sweating, and difficulty breathing. To help the client tolerate these experiences, the client is MOST LIKELY to be prescribed:

A. Risperidone
B. Haloperidol
C. Amitriptyline
D. Alprazolam

161. A client is unable to obtain health insurance due to being undocumented. The client states she has put off addressing health issues because she cannot afford the cost of doctor visits and prescriptions. To BEST help this client obtain needed care, the social worker should:

A. Connect the client with health care clinics that offer free or low-cost services
B. Conduct a community needs assessment
C. Connect the client with an immigration attorney

162. The purpose of follow-up after termination is to:

A. Encourage clients to return to treatment after goals have been met
B. Ensure that clients have followed up on any referrals, and to find out if any new needs have arisen
C. Convey that the treatment relationship is open-ended
D. Address an agency's business development needs

163. In client-centered therapy, the therapist's genuineness and openness in communication with clients is referred to as:

A. Unconditional positive regard
B. Congruence
C. Accurate empathic understanding

164. A client meets with a social worker in an agency setting. The client appears angry and withdrawn. When asked about this, the client states that he is very angry with the social worker. The social worker recently returned from vacation, and the client describes thinking that the social worker has taken an excessive number of vacations in the past year. The client would like to speak with the agency director to provide feedback regarding staff vacation policies, as he feels that clients need staff to be there consistently. In response to the client's feelings, the social worker should do all of the following EXCEPT:

A. Acknowledge the client's feelings
B. Inform the client of agency processes for receiving client feedback
C. Remind the client that he was informed in advance about the social worker's vacation
D. Explore the client's experience during the time that the social worker was away

165. In meeting with a social worker, a client describes being overwhelmed at all she has to do. The client is changing jobs and moving, all while planning to become a first-time parent. The social worker explores which tasks are overwhelming to the client, and helps the client to divide these issues into more manageable units. The social worker is using the technique of:

A. Interpreting
B. Partializing
C. Reflecting

166. A psychiatric hospital social worker is a member of a multidisciplinary team and regularly gives case presentations at team meetings. In preparing a case presentation, the social worker is likely to include all of the following EXCEPT:

A. Assessment
B. Diagnosis
C. Process recordings
D. Treatment plan

167. Which of the following medications is LEAST likely to cause sexual side effects?

A. Prozac
B. Zoloft
C. Wellbutrin

168. All of the following are indicators of positive ego strength EXCEPT:

A. Egocentrism
B. Tolerance of disappointment
C. Compassion toward others
D. Flexibility

169. A Black client visits a county social services department to submit an application for food assistance benefits. At the office, he is kept waiting for over an hour, only to be told that his paperwork is incomplete and that he will need to come back later. When the client's White social worker visits that same office, the social worker is greeted immediately by the same employee that the client had spoken to and is able to submit the client's paperwork exactly as the client had filled it out previously. The experience of the social worker is MOST LIKELY a result of:

A. White privilege
B. Gender stereotypes
C. Inclusion

170. A 25 year old client meets with a social worker and states that he has been experiencing stomach pain for the past 6 months. He has visited several medical professionals, who could find no physical cause for the client's pain. The client describes feeling very anxious about his symptoms, as he worries they may be signs of cancer. He thinks about this often and has difficulty functioning at work as a result. The client's likely DSM-5 diagnosis is:

A. Somatic symptom disorder
B. Fibromyalgia
C. Schizophrenia
D. Factitious disorder

Practice Exam Answers and Explanations

1. **B.** This action is unethical, as the social worker should not prioritize their own self-interest over the interests of the client. According to the *NASW Code of Ethics*, social workers' primary responsibility is to promote client well-being. Clients' interests are, in general, the primary focus. The *Code of Ethics* further states that social workers are not to take unfair advantage of a professional relationship, nor should social workers exploit others for their own interests. In this example, the social worker's attempt to have the client include the social worker in his will would constitute taking unfair advantage as well as financial exploitation.

2. **B.** The use of rating scales before the start of the intervention would be considered the pretest. Pretest-posttest designs are used in experimental and quasi-experimental research and involve taking measurements both before and after the intervention being studied. The pretest refers to preliminary measures administered in advance of an intervention in order to establish a baseline level. Posttest measures, on the other hand, are measurements administered after the study intervention, which collect data for comparison with the pretest results.

3. **B.** The social worker should decline the connection request. According to the *NASW Code of Ethics*, social workers should not accept requests from clients on social networking sites. This is to prevent boundary confusion, dual relationships, and potential harm. While this request is from a former client rather than from a current client, the same principles would apply as it is still important to prevent dual relationships with former clients.

4. **A.** The client's most likely DSM-5 diagnosis is histrionic personality disorder. Histrionic personality disorder is a mental health disorder in which the person exhibits dramatic behavior and experiences an overwhelming desire to be noticed, recognized, and appreciated. For individuals with histrionic personality disorder, attention seeking behaviors typically begin in early childhood. Individuals may exhibit inappropriate seductive behaviors, and often experience a strong desire for the approval of others. This may be caused by a distorted self-image and low self-worth. For people with histrionic personality disorder, treatment may involve various types of therapy including psychodynamic psychotherapy, cognitive-behavioral therapy (CBT), and interpersonal therapy (IPT).

5. **D.** The client is in the pre-contemplation stage of the transtheoretical model. In the pre-contemplation stage, the person does not yet acknowledge that there is a problem that needs to

be changed. The person may justify the problem behavior and may react defensively when others point out the problem or recommend that the person change their behavior. During this stage, the person is not actively seeking help for the problem behavior, but may still encounter a social worker in a clinical setting.

6. **D.** The social worker should refer the client to a colleague who has expertise in treating clients with psychotic disorders. According to the *NASW Code of Ethics*, social workers are required to refer clients to other professionals when those professionals' expertise is necessary based on the needs of the client. Further, the *Code of Ethics* states that social workers should provide services only within their areas of competence based on their education and professional experience. In this case, treating a client with schizophrenia requires substantial training and experience, which this social worker does not have, and therefore the best option is to refer to another professional.

7. **C.** One purpose of supervision in social work practice is to assist the social worker in addressing issues of countertransference. When countertransference issues arise, the social worker should discuss them in supervision in order to process the social worker's reactions while remaining available to meet the needs of the client and maintaining appropriate professional boundaries. While supervision does often have an administrative component, supervision should not focus primarily on administrative tasks. Supervision is necessary both for student interns and for social work professionals, and can be provided by licensed social workers as well as by other mental health professionals. For example, depending on state regulations, supervision hours may count toward clinical licensure when provided by licensed psychologists or board-certified psychiatrists.

8. **C.** The process described in this example is groupthink. Groupthink is a psychological phenomenon in which group decision-making produces an irrational or dysfunctional outcome as a result of group members' tendency to minimize conflict based on a desire for harmony and conformity. In this case, team members do not feel comfortable expressing their doubts, and instead pursue a course of action based on the apparent group consensus without considering alternatives.

9. **B.** While dual relationships create the potential for many problems, they cannot and should not be avoided 100% of the time. Dual or multiple relationships occur when a social worker relates to clients in more than one role, which may be professional, social, and/or business. Dual relationships can create the potential for boundary crossing, and can pose ethical concerns. Because of this, dual or multiple relationships are at times unethical. According to the *NASW Code of Ethics*, social workers should not engage in dual or multiple relationships with current or former clients when they pose a risk of exploitation or harm. At the same time, dual or multiple relationships are at times unavoidable, and must be navigated with clear, appropriate, and culturally sensitive boundaries.

10. **B.** The social worker should begin by conducting a needs assessment. In the community needs assessment process, the social worker will identify assets and needs in the community that the social

worker can help to mobilize for improvement and change. This will include an identification of the gaps in services that can be filled to meet the community's needs. After conducting the community needs assessment, the social worker should then establish a planning team or task force, define the goals and objectives of the program, develop an action plan, and implement that action plan.

11. **B.** A small sample size in a research study limits the generalizability of the results to the larger population. The smaller the sample size, the lower the likelihood that the sample is representative of that larger population. As a result, there is a greater potential for the characteristics of the larger population to be different from those of the small sample that is studied. However, the sample size does not impact the validity nor the reliability of the measurement tools that are used. The correlation coefficient can still be correctly calculated for any relationships that are studied between data points, and will refer only to the data that is collected for the sample under study.

12. **C.** The concrete operational stage in Piaget's theory of cognitive development occurs from the ages of 7 to 11 years, and is associated with the child's development of organized, rational thinking. One aspect of rational thought that children develop during this time is the concept of *conservation*. Conservation is the principle that the amount of something (whether in quantity, mass, volume, or length) will stay the same even as its appearance or distribution changes. For example, water poured from a short, wide glass into a tall, narrow glass will retain its volume even though it may look as though there is more water in the tall, narrow glass. Object permanence is the child's ability to understand that objects still exist even when the child cannot see or hear them. Object permanence is developed during the sensorimotor stage of development. Animism is the ascribing of life characteristics to inanimate objects. For example, the child may believe that a stuffed teddy bear has feelings. Animism is associated with the pre-operational stage of cognitive development. Egocentrism, in Piaget's theory, refers to a young child's inability to see things from another person's point of view, and the inability to understand that another person's perspective may be different from one's own. Egocentrism is associated with the pre-operational stage of cognitive development.

13. **A.** The social worker should explore the clinical implications of attending or not attending the client's graduation ceremony. While the social worker has no obligation to attend, and can decline based on their own personal limits, attendance at a client's significant life event is generally permissible and ethical if handled with sensitive and appropriate boundaries. If a social worker does attend a client's life event, it should be at the request of the client and the therapist must be careful to maintain confidentiality of the social worker - client relationship.

14. **C.** The type of research described involves the use of grounded theory. Grounded theory is an approach to qualitative research that begins with collecting observations and involves looking for patterns and themes that emerge from those observations. This involves the application of inductive reasoning rather than deductive reasoning.

15. **D.** This case example describes the use of denial as a defense mechanism. Denial is one of the most common defense mechanisms, and involves ignoring the reality of a situation in order to protect oneself from the uncomfortable feelings that the situation involves. Denial keeps a person from addressing a problem and making needed changes. In this case, the client's cocaine use is causing negative consequences in his life, yet he has not yet acknowledged this due to denial.

16. **D.** The researcher's erroneous belief is a causal fallacy. A causal fallacy is a logical error in which one concludes that an event that occurs first is the cause of an event that follows. There are several types of causal fallacies, the most common of which is the correlation/causation error. The distribution of umbrellas did not, of course, cause it to rain, even though these data points are closely related (correlated). Rather, it is more likely that the umbrellas were distributed due to a forecast of rainy weather and/or due to the observation of rain.

17. **D.** Informed consent is the process by which a client grants a social worker and/or agency permission to use specific interventions. Informed consent should be based on a full disclosure of all information the client will need in order to make this decision. An informed consent document should include the purpose of the proposed treatment, risks of the proposed treatment, and any alternatives to the proposed treatment. This allows clients to decide for themselves whether or not they would like to proceed.

18. **A.** The child's behavior is indicative of secure attachment. Secure attachment, one of the four main attachment styles in attachment theory, refers to a healthy and strong bond between the child and their caregiver. Securely attached children show signs of distress when the caregiver leaves, but are quickly comforted by the caregiver's return. Children with secure attachment feel protected by their caregiver and trust that the caregiver will return. In this case example, the child is distressed by the fathers' departure, but is comforted by their return at the end of the school day.

19. **D.** Best practices for addressing burnout include practicing self-care, engaging in mindfulness activities, and connecting with other professionals. Further, a multi-faceted approach is often needed in cases of burnout, and so the correct answer is all of the above. Burnout takes the forms of depletion or exhaustion, increased distancing mentally from one's professional role, negativity or cynicism toward one's work, and reduced effectiveness in a professional role. Addressing burnout requires both structural and individual changes. At the individual level, addressing burnout requires multiple, ongoing forms of self-care (i.e., a lifestyle rather than a vacation), including mindfulness, along with engagement with a community of colleagues.

20. **B.** The concept of "duty to warn" refers to a mental health professional's obligation to inform potential victims, as well as the appropriate authorities, when a client threatens to physically harm others. In the United States, the concept of duty to warn comes from case law, specifically

Tarasoff v. Regents of the University of California. Similarly, in Canada, courts have found that the duty to warn others of imminent danger can outweigh professionals' responsibility to maintain client confidentiality.

21. **B.** The social worker described in this example is utilizing principles of evidence-based practice. Evidence-based practice is a process for integrating evidence with clinical expertise and values to select effective interventions to help clients. In considering the client's diagnosis and demographic information, and reviewing professional literature about this diagnosis and population, the social worker is determining which interventions have been proven effective based on the available evidence. The social worker then makes practice decisions based on the evidence, hence the term evidence-based practice.

22. **A.** The child has not yet developed conservation, which is the understanding that objects can change in appearance but still retain the same quantity, size, or volume. Conservation would allow an older child to understand that the sandwich can be cut any way and still retain the same amount of food. A common "conservation task" is to pour water from a short, wide glass into a tall, narrow glass and ask the child which glass contains more water. With the theory of conservation, the child will understand that both contain the same amount of water even though the tall, narrow glass may look like it contains more. According to Piaget, the development of conservation occurs during the concrete operational stage of cognitive development.

23. **C.** Social work student interns should not identify themselves as social workers when providing services to clients, but rather should identify themselves as student interns. According to the *NASW Code of Ethics*, social workers should accurately represent their education and credentials to clients, agencies, and the public. Therefore, it is important for student interns to inform clients of this status. Student interns should also inform clients of when their field practicum will end, in order to prepare clients for termination, and should also inform clients of their supervision arrangement so that clients are aware of what information will be shared and with whom.

24. **B.** According to Erikson's stages of psychosocial development, the stage of trust vs. mistrust occurs from an infant's birth up to 18 months of age. During the trust vs. mistrust stage, infants are tasked with creating a basic sense of trust in themselves and in their environments. However, with unreliable care, the infant may experience a sense of loss, leading to feelings of mistrust that can continue throughout life. Therefore, the social worker's intervention in this case should be to assist the infant in developing a sense of trust through placement with a reliable caregiver.

25. **C.** Environmental justice refers to the principle of fair treatment of all people with regard to environmental policies, making sure that no group is forced to bear a disproportionate burden of environmental problems and risks. In this case, low-income residents and people of color are facing

disproportionate consequences of poor air quality, and so the social worker is helping the most impacted residents to advocate for change.

26. **A.** Major depressive disorder is diagnosed in clients who have experienced symptoms for a period of 2 weeks or longer. To make a diagnosis of major depressive disorder, the client must experience five or more symptoms during the same 2 week period, including depressed mood or loss of interest or pleasure in all or almost all activities. Other possible symptoms include weight loss or weight gain, slowing down of thought and/or physical movement, fatigue, feelings of worthlessness or inappropriate guilt, difficulty concentrating, and thoughts of death and/or suicidal ideation.

27. **A.** The client's most likely diagnosis is Bipolar I disorder. For a diagnosis of Bipolar I disorder, the client must have experienced at least one manic episode. Most individuals with bipolar I disorder also experience major depressive episodes, but this is not a requirement for the diagnosis. The client's period of 8 days in which he was irritable, stayed up throughout the night for several nights out of the week, incurred significant credit card debt, and engaged in unprotected sex with multiple partners represents a manic episode. This manic episode is distinguishable from a hypomanic episode in that manic episodes are severe enough to cause impairment in social and occupational functioning, while hypomanic episodes are not.

28. **C.** The social worker's role in this situation is to advocate for the student to receive the services that they need from the school. In the United States, the Individuals with Disabilities Education Act (IDEA) requires that students with disabilities be provided with a free and appropriate public education tailored to their specific needs. IDEA requires the development of an Individualized Education Program (IEP) for students with disabilities as well as placement in the least restrictive environment possible. Since this student has not received the services and support that the school is required to provide, advocacy is the appropriate next step. Social workers do not provide psychometric testing in schools, but may advocate for this testing if it is needed.

29. **C.** Stakeholders is a term that refers to any person or group that has an interest in an organization's activities or resources, or that is affected by the organization's work. Because the social worker is engaged in advocacy efforts to address the needs of the local indigenous population, the social worker's client system is the local indigenous community rather than the specific individuals with whom she interacts.

30. **B.** Devolution is a process by which the responsibility for social welfare programs is shifted from the national (federal) government to state, provincial, or local governments. Devolution has resulted in significant changes to how social service programs are administered, and has caused the closing of small community-based organizations as local social service providers compete for limited resources.

31. **C.** This is a recall question. Pansexual is a sexual orientation identity defined by a person's sexual and/or romantic attraction to people regardless of sex or gender. Pansexuality is different from bisexuality in that the term bisexual may imply attraction to both men and women, while pansexual is a label inclusive of more than 2 sexes and genders. Individuals who experience sexual attraction only in the context of a strong emotional connection may identify with the term demisexual.

32. **B.** The person's experience most closely reflects disparate treatment. Disparate treatment is discriminatory, unfavorable treatment based on an individual's personal characteristics such as age, race, sex, gender identity or expression, sexual orientation, or disability. In this case, the employee is assigned less desirable tasks than her male colleagues and passed over for promotions in a way that appears to be based on her gender.

33. **C.** According to psychoanalytic theory, neurosis is a chronic state of fear or anxiety that causes distress and difficulty in functioning, but does not result in delusions, hallucinations, or other difficulties in reality testing. Neurosis describes a wide range of symptoms and is distinct from psychosis.

34. **A.** Social determinants of health are conditions in people's living environments that affect a wide range of health, functioning, and quality of life factors. Examples of social determinants of health include racism, discrimination, job opportunities, access to healthy food and exercise, air quality, and water quality. For example, individuals with limited economic resources due to unemployment or low wages are less likely to have access to healthy food, and less likely to have outdoor spaces conducive to physical activity, resulting in higher rates of diabetes. Similarly, when sources of air pollution are located in neighborhoods with low-income residents, those residents are likely to have higher rates of asthma as a result.

35. **C.** Empowerment practices, based on empowerment theory, focus on power in order to reduce inequity and support equity. Empowerment is used to counteract experiences of power-lessness by positioning marginalized people as the experts of their own experience. In social work practice, empowerment involves collaborating with clients to develop solutions and connecting clients to community resources. In this case, the social worker supports clients in finding their own solutions and in developing a sense of community at the group level.

36. **D.** Intersectionality theory recognizes the ways in which various aspects of identity have combined effects on a person's experiences in life based on the ways in which each identity is associated with oppression and/or privilege. In this example, the social worker asks the client about their experiences with oppression and privilege with regard to various social identities in order to explore their intersecting effects.

37. **C.** In working with a multidisciplinary team in the school setting, social workers provide a psychosocial perspective based on their assessment of the student's strengths and service needs. Social workers should also use teamwork skills to collaborate effectively with other professionals as well as to engage the student and family as partners in the Individualized Education Program process.

38. **B.** Deductive reasoning, also referred to as hypothetical-deductive reasoning or the hypothetical-deductive method, is a "top-down" approach in which an individual begins with a hypothesis or theory, and then tests whether or not their observations fit with this hypothesis or theory. In this way, they can reason based on general principles in order to determine specific facts. Deductive reasoning is associated with Piaget's formal operational stage of cognitive development, which begins at the age of 12 years. Once they develop this ability, children can test hypotheses and draw conclusions from their findings.

39. **A.** According to Freud's structural theory of personality, the human mind consists of three parts: the id, the ego, and the superego. The id represents the person's natural instincts, while the superego is the critical and moralizing part of the self and the ego serves a mediating function between the other two parts. Working together, these three components create the complexity of human behavior and experience. Freud describes the id as driven by the pleasure principle, seeking immediate gratification of desires and needs. This fits with the description of the client in this question, who feels he must seek pleasure at all costs and satisfy impulses immediately.

40. **B.** Clients often have multiple goals and needs, and Maslows' need theory (often described as the hierarchy of needs) gives us a framework for prioritizing. While the client describes wanting to become the best possible version of himself (akin to self-actualization in Maslow's hierarchy), he also has other needs that will need to be met before he can achieve this stated goal. The client is unemployed, wishes to establish longer-lasting and more meaningful friendships, and also has limited access to food. Of these, access to food is needed to meet the first level of Maslow's hierarchy, which consists of physiological needs.

41. **C.** This question asks specifically about the use of client-centered therapy (also known as person-centered therapy), which was developed by Carl Rogers. Two key principles of client-centered therapy are unconditional positive regard and the use of accurate empathetic understanding. Unconditional positive regard involves a nondirective, nonjudgmental therapist showing complete support and acceptance of the client. Accurate empathic understanding, according to Rogers, is more than a reflection of feelings. It involves an in-the-moment presence and attunement to the client's feelings and experiences.

42. **A.** While all of the answer choices are true, the question asks specifically why conversion therapy is considered to be harmful. Conversion therapy is harmful because it has been found

to increase suicidal ideation and other negative mental health outcomes in clients who have been subjected to this pseudoscientific practice. Because of these harms, conversion therapy is considered unethical by all major mental health organizations and has been made illegal in many jurisdictions. Still, the practice remains politically controversial.

43. **A.** The social worker is most likely applying the principles of positive psychology. Positive psychology focuses on ideas of optimism, resilience, hope, and motivation. In this way, it is consistent with the strengths perspective in social work. In this case, the social worker seeks to increase the client's sense of happiness and experience of well-being, focusing on increasing desired emotions and activities rather than focusing on the client's problems or symptoms.

44. **C.** This question asks specifically about the use of the strengths perspective. In using the strengths perspective, the social worker should identify the client's internal and external resources in order to support resilience. The strengths perspective does not focus on targeting specific symptoms but rather focuses on client assets or strengths. Similarly, client deficits or pathology would not be a focus of treatment in this model.

45. **C.** Erikson's stage of autonomy vs. shame and doubt occurs from 18 months of age to 3 years of age. During this stage, the toddler is tasked with gaining a sense of self-control and developing the virtue of will. Children in this stage assert their desire for independence and greater control over themselves and their surroundings. Toilet training typically occurs during this stage, and developing control over bodily functions gives children feelings of control and independence.

46. **C.** The concept of resilience refers to an individual or community's ability to overcome difficult experiences and risks in order to "bounce back" and adapt to challenging circumstances. Resilience at the individual level is associated with coping, self-efficacy, and competence; it is consistent with a social work strengths perspective. Community resilience, similarly, refers to the process of coping and recovery in communities faced with collective stress and trauma.

47. **A.** The school social worker and teacher are using the approach of behavioral modification. Based on operant conditioning, behavioral modification involves the use of positive reinforcement and modeling along with, to a lesser extent, punishment for undesired behaviors. In this example, the social worker assists the teacher in applying concepts of reinforcement and modeling from behavioral theory in order to improve the child's functioning in school.

48. **D.** Biopsychosocial assessment is an aspect of direct social work practice (i.e., clinical social work) but not an aspect of community organization. *Biopsychosocial assessment* is the predominant assessment framework used in clinical social work practice, including both psychotherapy and case management, and refers to a holistic consideration of the physical, mental, emotional, and environmental factors that impact a person's experience and behavior. Social action, locality development,

and social planning are all types of community organization practices. *Social action* refers to collective efforts directed toward a shared goal, such as addressing macro level problems and conditions in a community or society. *Locality development* involves community-driven efforts to improve the quality of community life for residents in a neighborhood, such as by developing programs and services and building community support systems. *Social planning* is a term that describes the fact-finding process of determining the social problems that need to be addressed in the community and identifying possible solutions.

49. **A.** The social worker should first conduct a comprehensive biopsychosocial assessment in order to most effectively determine the client's needs. As this is an initial session, the social worker's focus should be on engagement and assessment. Consulting with family caregivers for collateral information may be a component of this assessment process, but should not replace the client interview nor a full exploration of the biological, psychological, and social factors affecting the client. Only after the biopsychosocial assessment should treatment planning and then interventions take place.

50. **B.** Upon hiring a new employee, a social work administrator should review the job description with the employee and provide them with a copy of it. In a human resource management role, which this administrator is in, social workers should use a person-in-environment perspective in working with employees and should use best practices to promote organizational effectiveness and equity. The use of job descriptions is one way to ensure that employees know what is expected of them, as well as to reduce bias in the hiring process.

51. **B.** Rational emotive behavior therapy (REBT), developed by Albert Ellis, is a type of cognitive behavioral therapy that utilizes the "ABC" model to help clients identify activating events, beliefs, and consequences (emotional responses). In this example, the social worker assists the client in identifying events that activate her irrational beliefs, which in turn produce an anxiety response.

52. **C.** Identity vs. role confusion is the stage of Erikson's psychosocial development theory that is associated with the adolescent years (12-18 years of age). During this stage, adolescents experiment with roles and behaviors in order to develop a sense of self. It is normal for adolescents to struggle with how to identify themselves in terms of ethnicity, culture, ideology, sexual orientation, gender, and other social identities. In this case, the adolescent's experience as an Afghan refugee living in the United States plays a significant role in her identity formation.

53. **A.** The social worker in an administrative and supervisory role should not engage in dual relationships with supervisees. According to the *NASW Code of Ethics*, social workers providing supervision or consultation should not engage in dual or multiple relationships that pose potential harm to the supervisee. In addition, social work supervisors must set clear, appropriate, and

culturally sensitive boundaries. The *Code of Ethics* also states that social workers should provide supervision only within their areas of knowledge and competence.

54. **A.** The question asks specifically about the steps of the helping process, and the social worker is currently in the engagement and assessment phases of work with this client. While the social worker appears to already have some information about the client's condition, the next step is to conduct a comprehensive biopsychosocial-cultural-spiritual assessment. Only once this assessment has been completed should the planning and intervention steps of the helping process take place.

55. **D.** The social worker should first discuss these concerns with the colleague directly. According to the *NASW Code of Ethics*, social workers who become aware that a colleague is impaired due to substance abuse, mental health problems, or other personal problems should speak directly with that colleague when feasible in order to assist the colleague in addressing the issue. Only once this has been done, and if the colleague has not taken steps to address this impairment, should a social worker take action through other channels.

56. **A.** The stress-diathesis model represents a theory of dynamic exchange between a person's genes, their environment, and human behavior. While a person may have a genetic predisposition to mental health disorders, a person's environment (such as exposure to significant stressors) affects the expression of these genes. At the biological level, this has been studied through evaluation of the effects of the stress hormone cortisol. Thus, in the stress-diathesis model, mental health disorders are not considered to be caused exclusively by either the person's genetics or their environment, but rather by the interactions between both of these factors.

57. **C.** The client's most likely diagnosis is body dysmorphic disorder. Body dysmorphic disorder is a mental condition in which the individual is distressed by obsessive thoughts about one or more perceived flaws or defects in their physical appearance that are not apparent to others, or that would appear only slight to others.

58. **A.** The social work researcher is using inductive reasoning. An inductive approach involves using observations and experiences to create new theories. Inductive reasoning is typically used in qualitative research methods, which favor observation and interviewing and seek to describe the complexity of people's experiences. Inductive reasoning can be contrasted with deductive reasoning (also called the hypothetico-deductive method), which begins with a hypothesis that is tested in order to support or falsify a theory.

59. **B.** Mood refers to a person's subjective experience of their own feeling state. In a mental status exam, the clinician will typically ask the client how they are feeling and quote this description verbatim as the client's mood.

60. **B.** When conducting couples therapy, it is especially important that social workers are attentive to issues of confidentiality. Unless disclosure is mandated due to imminent risk, child abuse or neglect, or a court order, social workers should not disclose information collected in couples therapy without the consent of both partners. In addition, social workers should discuss with clients how confidentiality will be handled if one partner shares information with the therapist outside of the couples' sessions.

61. **C.** To determine the optimal location for this outreach program, the social worker should conduct a needs assessment. Needs assessments are used to understand community needs and problems, and to help an agency develop and shape programs to meet community needs and address existing problems. More broadly, a community needs assessment can also identify a community's assets and strengths that can be used to mobilize the community for changes that improve residents' quality of life.

62. **C.** To help the client access the care that he needs, the social worker should first assess the client's eligibility for insurance coverage that will cover long-term care services. As the results of the social worker's assessment, and the recommendations of other treating providers, indicate that long-term care services are needed, the social worker should first explore the options most likely to make it possible for the client to access these services.

63. **C.** From the age of 18 months to 3 years, toddlers are navigating the psychosocial stage, or "crisis," of autonomy versus shame and doubt. During this stage, toddlers are tasked with gaining a sense of self-control and developing the virtue of will. Children in this stage assert their desire for independence and greater control over themselves and their surroundings. As part of this, throwing of tantrums and refusal to follow directions are normal during this stage.

64. **A.** Having completed the assessment and having found that the client meets criteria for a mental health disorder, the social worker should next develop a plan in collaboration with the client that includes both case management and mental health treatment services. In a prison setting, case management is an important service, especially for clients with mental health or substance use disorders. Mental health treatment should also be provided, which may include psychotherapy, medication management, or both.

65. **B.** The social worker should conduct a suicide risk assessment. Veterans, as well as anyone with depressive symptoms or symptoms that suggest possible post-traumatic stress disorder, are at elevated risk for suicide. The client's statement, "I can't take it anymore and I want to find a way out of this" may imply suicidal ideation and so the social worker should address this and determine the client's risk, in order to conduct safety planning if appropriate.

66. **B.** The client's feelings are most likely a result of trauma bonding. The concept of trauma bonding describes the emotional attachment that forms between an abuser and a victim. Trauma bonds have been found to form in a wide range of exploitive relationships. Victims experience abuse, control, and dependency on the one hand, while also experiencing love, admiration, and gratitude for the abuser at the same time.

67. **A.** The social worker should refer the client experiencing pain to a physician for a medical evaluation. When a condition may be caused by physical problems, a referral should first be made to determine any medical cause and ensure that the client receives necessary medical treatment. Only once this has been done should the condition be treated through psychotherapy. Similarly, a referral to a sex therapy specialist or the use of any therapy intervention is not appropriate until possible medical causes have been addressed.

68. **B.** The questions that this couple is being asked are examples of microaggressions. Micro-aggressions are subtly coded instances of discriminatory acts or speech that target individuals and groups based on race, religion, gender, sexual orientation, class, disability, and other identities. In contrast to overt aggression, microaggressions are thinly veiled and thus often free the perpetrator from accountability. Microaggressions take the form of microassaults, microinsults, and micro-invalidations.

69. **D.** A social worker should not terminate services in order to pursue a business relationship with a client. According to the *NASW Code of Ethics*, section 1.17(d), "Social workers should not terminate services to pursue a social, financial, or sexual relationship with a client." Termination of services should take place when the goals of treatment have been met and when new goals have not been identified. Other reasons a social worker may initiate termination include referral to a provider who can better meet the client's needs, and in certain instances of non-payment. If a client may need to change providers due to a change in insurance coverage, the social worker should discuss available options with the client and support the client in making an informed decision. When terminating services due to non-payment, the social worker must inform the client of the balance due, discuss the consequences of non-payment with the client, and ensure that the client does not pose a danger to themself or others.

70. **D.** The client's most likely DSM-5 diagnosis is adjustment disorder. Adjustment disorder involves clinically significant symptoms that occur in response to an identifiable stressor, occur within 3 months of the stressor, have not lasted for more than 6 months following the termination of the stressor and its consequences, and that do not meet criteria for another mental health disorder. The DSM-5 further notes that normal bereavement responses do not meet the criteria for a diagnosis of adjustment disorder.

71. **A.** One clinical advantage of short-term treatment as compared to long-term treatment is that having a known termination date can motivate both the client and the social worker to mobilize their available resources in order to reach the client's goals. Both short-term and long-term models can include the use of evidence-based practice interventions and can be effective. While insurance plans may at times seek to limit the number of sessions a client can receive, parity laws require insurance plans that cover mental health services to cover such services to the same extent that they cover physical health services, without any treatment limitations that are more restrictive than those placed on physical health services.

72. **A.** According to the strengths perspective, social workers should assist clients in identifying their inner resources and assets, and assist the client in accessing those resources and assets to meet their goals. This approach presents an alternative to the common focus on client's problems and dysfunctional behaviors. The strengths perspective also incorporates cultural and personal narratives, as well as the use of family and community resources. In this way, problems and difficulties can be seen as opportunities for clients to learn new skills and grow.

73. **B.** The agency should not exclude clients with mental health disorders. Clients with mental health disorders can receive home visits and are likely to benefit from this service. At the same time, attending to worker safety is important for any agency and has specific importance in the provision of home visits. Best practices for attending to worker safety include conducting a thorough clinical risk assessment for each client, providing high quality safety training for workers, and convening an agency safety committee in order to oversee the implementation of safe workplace strategies.

74. **A.** The dynamic between this mother and her older daughter reflects enmeshment. The mother's behavior of confiding in her daughter and relying on her emotionally reflects a diffusion of boundaries, which may cause the daughter to become focused on her mother's needs rather than on her own growth and identity development. Enmeshment is common in families affected by alcoholism.

75. **B.** The social worker's behavior is most reflective of anticipatory empathy. Anticipatory empathy refers to the use of understanding about another person to predict the likely impact of one's words or actions on that other person. Social workers can prepare to enter into a client's world by considering facts about the client's life and using anticipatory empathy to consider the client's likely feelings and experiences.

76. **C.** The client does not meet criteria for a mental health disorder at this time but rather has uncomplicated bereavement, which is listed in the DSM-5 as a condition (but not a disorder) that may be a focus of clinical attention. Uncomplicated bereavement is defined as a normal reaction to the death of a loved one, which may include symptoms that would otherwise indicate a major depressive episode. In uncomplicated bereavement, it is normal to experience sadness, insomnia,

low appetite, and weight loss. Individuals may seek (and receive) treatment for these symptoms even when they do not meet criteria for major depressive disorder.

77. **B.** The social worker should refer the client (in this case, the caseworker who was referred) for the level of care that he needs. Since the social worker is unable to provide the required level of care in this agency setting, the social worker should refer the client to a more appropriate setting. Treatment decisions should be based on the needs of the client, rather than on sessions authorized through a particular employee benefit.

78. **B.** The social worker is engaged in community organizing. In this case, the social worker performs the role of facilitator, supporting neighborhood residents to advocate for themselves and pursue change in their community. Community organizing uses both conflict and consensus approaches, helping people to understand their shared problems and to work together toward solutions. Community organizing seeks to build on social connections to support collective action in a sustainable way. Community organizing can take various forms including social planning, social action, and social development.

79. **B.** This is a recall question. In the life model of social work practice, the concept of habitat refers to rural or urban environments including residences, workplaces, and public amenities. Based on ecological and life course theories, the life model of social work is an approach that seeks to improve the person-environment fit, particularly with regard to human needs and available resources. Through their impact on person-in-environment transactions, human habitats can support or impede adaptive functioning in families and communities.

80. **B.** Conversion disorder, also known as functional neurological symptom disorder, is a mental health disorder in which the individual experiences altered voluntary motor or sensory function, which cannot be explained by any medical condition. For a diagnosis of conversion disorder, it is necessary for the client to be assessed to rule out neurological disease. While conversion disorder is categorized among the somatic symptom and related disorders, it is distinct from somatic symptom disorder. Somatic symptom disorder is defined by the distress or preoccupation that a person experiences based on physical symptoms, even as it is also a condition that involves physical symptoms for which no medical cause can be found.

81. **B.** The client's most likely DSM-5 diagnosis is factitious disorder. Factitious disorder is a mental health condition in which a person deceives other people by appearing sick, purposefully becoming sick, or injuring oneself. Factitious disorder is distinguished from malingering by the fact that those with factitious disorder do not receive clear external rewards in relation to their symptoms. With malingering, on the other hand, clients seek to achieve a specific goal such as financial gain, excusal from work, or to address legal issues. While factitious disorder is a DSM-5 mental disorder, malingering is not.

82. **A.** Receipt of a subpoena from an attorney is not an ethical reason to disclose client information without consent. A subpoena is not the same as a court order, and an attorney who is not a judge does not have the authority to compel the release of records. In response to a subpoena, a social worker should claim privilege and should not provide records unless a court order is issued. Even when in receipt of a court order, the social worker should attempt to limit the scope of records required, and should request that records remain under seal.

83. **B.** In this research study, the measurements taken following the termination of treatment are considered the posttest. Posttest measurements are assessment measures given to research participants following the administration of a treatment intervention as part of the study design. Pretest measurements, on the other hand, would be the assessment measures given to participants prior to the start of any intervention. In such a design, the intervention type and/or extent of intervention provided at a particular point would represent the independent variable(s), and the results of the assessment measures would represent the dependent variable(s).

84. **B.** SWOT analysis refers to an organizational study that seeks to identify the organization's strengths, weaknesses, opportunities, and threats. In conducting this analysis, an organization gains insight into issues that can be addressed through strategic planning. SWOT analysis is typically conducted by a strategic planning committee as a baseline assessment in order to understand the organization's internal resources and capacities, as well as outside forces that will affect the organization going forward. In addition, a SWOT analysis will identify factors critical to the success of the organization as well as the organization's distinctive competencies.

85. **A.** This client would be considered an asylum seeker, or refugee, since she fled another country in order to escape persecution. Refugees are considered forced migrants, as they are victims of human rights violations, including war, and cannot return to their previous countries due to the risk of persecution. Refugees who are awaiting an official decision on their refugee status are considered asylum seekers.

86. **B.** Social workers' use of social media websites and applications creates the potential for boundary crossings. According to the *NASW Code of Ethics,* social workers should be aware of their personal affiliations and online presence, and how their involvement online may impact their ability to work effectively with particular clients. In addition, social workers should not accept connection or friend requests from clients, and should not engage in personal relationships with clients on social media. However, social workers may use social media in professional ways without engaging in direct communication with clients.

87. **A.** The social worker is engaging in community education. By providing information to the wider community about the services being offered and the population that the program will

serve, the social worker is addressing the opposition that has been voiced and that could potentially threaten the program's future. Community education is an aspect of community organizing and development, and involves efforts to help the public understand a social problem. Community education can serve a range of functions, including advocacy and health promotion. In this case, the social worker's efforts would not be considered psychoeducation as psychoeducation is a therapeutic intervention for clients and their families.

88. **C.** The social worker is using a convenience sampling method. A convenience sample is a sample selected based on availability. Often, in social work research, it is impractical or cost-prohibitive to create a random sample from the entire population of interest. For this reason, convenience sampling is often used. Similarly, many psychological studies have been conducted using undergraduate college students as a convenience sample. With convenience sampling, there are potential limitations to the sample's representativeness of a larger population.

89. **C.** Change management is a process of continuing to revise and renew an organization's direction, structure, and capacities based on evolving needs of internal and external stakeholders. Stages of change management include problem identification, organizational analysis, proposal of a solution, and planning and managing change. Parallel process is not a stage of change management, but rather is a clinical term referring to an aspect of the social worker - supervisor relationship. Parallel process describes the ways in which the social worker's relationship with their supervisor impacts the social worker's relationship with clients. Similarly, a positive relationship between a supervisor and managers is associated with a positive relationship between the supervisor and the workers they supervise.

90. **B.** In this study, the type of intervention provided is the independent variable, while client recidivism rates are the dependent variable. An independent variable is defined as a condition or quantity that is changed or controlled by the experimenter. A dependent variable in a research study is a condition or quantity that is studied based on a hypothesis that it will change based upon the independent variable. In other words, the dependent variable is being studied through a change or changes made to the independent variable. In this study, the researcher changes the independent variable (introducing motivational interviewing as an alternative to treatment as usual) in order to study potential changes to the dependent variable (recidivism rates).

91. **D.** The best response is for the social worker to decline the former client's invitation. According to the *NASW Code of Ethics*, social workers should avoid engaging in dual or multiple relationships with clients when such dual or multiple relationships create the risk of exploitation or harm to the client. Further, social workers should not engage in sexual contact with current or former clients because of the potential harm that this would cause to the client. In this case, meeting for coffee or communicating through a mobile dating application would constitute a dual relationship and could imply the potential for a sexual relationship. Ideally, the social worker would

not respond at all through the app but would instead decline the request through more proper channels of communication. Even so, D is the best answer from the choices given.

92. **B.** An individual's mastery of Erikson's psychosocial stage of integrity vs. despair is associated with the virtue of wisdom. Each of Erikson's stages of psychosocial development is associated with a particular "virtue" that one achieves through adaptive resolution of the particular stage's psychosocial crisis. Erikson's stage of integrity vs. despair begins in older adulthood and continues through to the end of life. During this stage, individuals look back over their lives and evaluate their experiences. Integrity (in this case, referring to ego integrity) is developed when one evaluates their life as satisfying and meaningful. If, on the other hand, the individual sees their life as unsatisfying and if they have significant regrets, they may then experience a state of despair. Through successful resolution of this stage, wisdom is the strength or virtue that the individual develops.

93. **A.** The quality control measure that this question describes is assessing the survey measure for inter-rater reliability. Reliability is a research term that describes the consistency of responses to a measurement tool over time. Among the multiple types of reliability is inter-rater reliability. Inter-rater reliability describes the degree of agreement between multiple individuals who observe responses or phenomena and assign ratings or codes to their observations.

94. **B.** Praxis describes the uniting of theory and action. Praxis refers to action that is based on critical reflection on theoretical principles. It is a social justice principle advanced by Paulo Freire in his text *Pedagogy of the Oppressed*. Rather than keeping theory within the realm of academia and real-world practice separate from theoretical work, praxis is an approach that unites the two through reflection.

95. **D.** In statistical measures of central tendency, the concept of the mean refers to an average. For example, if participants' scores on a statistical measure are 10, 16, and 40, the mean would be 22. (The scores of 10, 16, and 40 are added together and create a sum of 66. That total of 66 is divided by the number of participants, which is 3, resulting in an average of 22).

96. **B.** This client is most likely experiencing caregiver stress, which results from the physical and emotional strain of caring for another person. When family members provide care to older adults or disabled family members, they face stressors that can pose risks to their physical, emotional, and mental health. For example, caregivers are at an increased risk of depression. However, long-term caregiving can have positive outcomes in addition to these potential negative ones. Research has found that positive feelings and rewarding experiences of caregiving can mediate its negative effects.

97. **C.** Professional codes of ethics, such as the *NASW Code of Ethics*, includes core values of the social work profession and ethical principles that social workers must follow. Codes of ethics do not provide a list of all possible ethical dilemmas, as there are always new situations that may occur

in specific contexts. As such, it is not possible to provide step-by-step instructions for what to do in particular situations. In ethical dilemmas, social workers must identify the ethical issues at stake in order to discern the appropriate course of action. Even so, codes of ethics do contain specific requirements, and ethical principles are, in this way, more than just recommendations.

98. **A.** The social worker should first validate the client's feelings. The question indicates that the client is meeting with a social worker and describing intense emotions related to problems in the world, in this case climate change and potential ecological disaster. The social worker's first response should be to engage with the client and respond to the feelings that have been raised. Ecological theories and the person-in-environment perspective do not refer to environmental issues in this sense, but rather to a person's social environment. While the social worker may obtain further education on environmental issues, or green social work, this would not be the most direct response to the client's feelings in the moment.

99. **B.** The client is likely having difficulty with the psychosocial stage, or crisis, of integrity vs. despair. In Erikson's stages of psychosocial development, the crisis of integrity vs. despair describes the typical developmental process of older adults from age 65 through to the end of life. Integrity refers to ego integrity, i.e., a sense of wholeness in one's self concept. Viewing one's life as satisfying and meaningful contributes to a sense of integrity. On the other hand, a sense of despair can arise from seeing one's life as unsatisfying or full of regrets, especially if it seems there is no longer time to make significant changes. A life review is a process of looking back over one's life, analyzing its themes and deriving meaning in one's life experiences. Social workers use a life review process with older adults to assist clients in developing a sense of meaning and in affirming meaningful aspects of their lives and identities.

100. **C.** While client self-determination is often a priority in social work practice, it is not always the main priority. This is because the social worker's obligation to the client must be balanced with the social worker's obligation to the larger society as well as certain legal obligations. In this way, there are times in which the social worker's responsibilities to the larger society or to the law will supersede the social worker's responsibilities to the client. For example, a social worker is required to report if a client has abused or neglected a child, or is at risk of harming themself or others. The other 3 statements are true: social workers are prohibited from having sex with current (and former) clients; dual relationships should be avoided when possible; and social workers should support policies that advance social justice.

101. **D.** The teacher's action of taking away recess time represents negative reinforcement. When determining whether an action functions as reinforcement or punishment, it is important to look at the impact (i.e., the actual function) rather than the intention. Reinforcement is a condition that increases a behavior, while punishment is a condition that decreases a behavior – regardless of what an individual may be trying to do. In instances of reinforcement or punishment, positive refers to

an addition or introduction; negative, on the other hand, refers to a subtraction or taking away. In this case, taking away recess time is a withdrawal of something, and so it is considered negative. Since this condition increases the student's behavior, it is considered punishment.

102. **C.** The impact of the disparity in this case example describes social determinants of health, structural inequality, and systems theory. Behavioral theory is not directly relevant to this example. Social determinants of health is a concept that describes life conditions, including larger systemic forces and institutions, that shape the conditions of people's lives and their health. Structural inequality refers to the ways in which institutions and larger systems are structured such that they perpetuate and maintain conditions of inequality. Systems theory describes the interdependent and interactive relationships and transactions among multiple levels of social systems, including individuals, families, groups, organizations, communities, and the larger society. In this case, systems theory is relevant as it recognizes the role of the social environment on the problems that individuals face.

103. **D.** The co-worker's comment is an example of a microaggression as it implies that children should be cared for by mothers and that the client's plans for parenthood require him to perform functions outside of his stated gender identity. Microaggressions are subtly coded instances of discriminatory acts or speech that target individuals and groups based on race, religion, gender, sexual orientation, class, disability, and other identities. In contrast to overt aggression, microaggressions are thinly veiled and thus often free the perpetrator from accountability. Microaggressions take the form of microassaults, microinsults, and microinvalidations.

104. **B.** The social worker's next action should be to seek cultural competency training and education relevant to Native American culture and specifically to the culture and customs of the tribe with which he is working. While asking clients about their cultural background and experiences is sometimes appropriate, this is not a next step in addressing a larger issue, in that this social worker is offending multiple clients and has found that he does not understand the cultural norms of the community in which he is working.

105. **A.** Grounded theory is an approach used in qualitative research, in which the researcher begins by making observations and then looks for patterns and themes that emerge from the data. The researcher then uses these patterns and themes to develop new theories that center the participants' lived experiences. While the example described could also be a component of a mixed methods study, there is no mention in the question stem of a quantitative component to the study. Thus, the best answer is that this is most likely a qualitative study.

106. **C.** The introduction of Antabuse (disulfiram) represents an aversive stimulus, and this treatment can be considered a type of aversion therapy or aversive conditioning. For a client with alcohol addiction, alcohol is a desired stimulus as drinking leads to the mental and physical sensations that the client has come to seek. With the introduction of the medication, which is an aversive

stimulus, the client experiences skin flushing, nausea, vomiting, headache, and other unpleasant physical reactions when they drink. When this treatment is effective, the client comes to associate drinking with these negative effects, developing a conditioned aversion to alcohol.

107. **D.** The research findings represent a curvilinear relationship. A curvilinear relationship describes a statistical correlation between two variables in which, as one variable increases, the other increases as well but only up to a certain level. After that point is reached, the relationship changes, such that as one variable increases the other variable decreases. In this case, workers who are assigned more tasks are more productive, but only to a point. If assigned too many tasks, they are less productive than they would be if their assignments had not crossed a certain threshold.

108. **B.** The social worker should report the suspected abuse to the local adult protective services agency. Social workers are legally mandated to report situations of elder abuse. Elder abuse reporting goes through state and local adult protective services (APS) agencies, which investigate and assess cases of suspected mistreatment of older adults as well as other vulnerable adults including abuse, neglect, and financial exploitation.

109. **D.** When working with clients who have experienced trauma, social workers should utilize principles of trauma-informed care. Trauma-informed care is based on the core principles of safety, trustworthiness, choice, collaboration, and empowerment. A trauma-informed approach includes establishing safety and stability, providing case management to meet basic needs, and addressing issues of grief and mourning related to the traumatic event. Exposure therapy is an evidence-based treatment for post-traumatic stress disorder, but exposure techniques such as imaginal exposure should only be utilized once the client has adequate coping skills and stability to manage the potential distress associated with exposure.

110. **B.** The social worker should use a stance of cultural humility. While cultural competence as a term implies a professional "knowing," cultural humility implies its opposite – not knowing. Instead of focusing on professional expertise or competence, cultural humility instead accepts that clients are far more knowledgeable about themselves and their experiences than practitioners can be. In this case, embracing a stance of cultural humility will lead the social worker to maintain self-awareness, a respectful attitude toward the client's cultural experience, and a valuing of the client's knowledge about their own experiences.

111. **C.** Fluoxetine, also known by the brand name Prozac, is a selective serotonin reuptake inhibitor (SSRI) and is commonly prescribed for depressive and anxiety disorders. Lithium, occasionally known by the brand name Lithobid, is a mood stabilizer and is commonly prescribed for bipolar disorder. Risperidone, also known by the brand names Risperdal and Perseris, is an antipsychotic medication used to treat schizophrenia and bipolar disorder. Venlafaxine, also known by the brand

name Effexor, is an antidepressant and is classified as a serotonin-norepinephrine reuptake inhibitor (SNRI).

112. **B.** Program evaluations can take the form of needs assessments, process evaluations, outcome evaluations, or cost-efficiency evaluations. In this case, the funding agency is requesting data demonstrating the effectiveness of the funded services. This objective would be best met through an outcome evaluation. Practice evaluation seeks to assess the effectiveness of the practice interventions of a particular social worker with a particular client, and so it would not support the effectiveness of an entire program. Single-case design, or single-system design, is the research approach used in practice evaluation; program evaluation instead uses a group design. While a randomized controlled trial is an excellent method for evaluating the effectiveness of an intervention, it is unlikely to be used in this case due to cost and practical reasons.

113. **C.** The social worker should first acknowledge the husband's feelings. The couple is meeting with the social worker presumably for the first time, or at least for the first time with this particular presenting problem. Therefore, the focus should be on engagement with the client or client system. Based on the husband's disclosure, the social worker should meet him where he is and respond to the feelings he has expressed. After this engagement need has been addressed, the social worker can then proceed with assessment-focused questions in order to determine how to best help the couple.

114. **B.** In assessing community needs in the context of a local senior center, the social worker is practicing at the mezzo level. Micro-level social work involves direct clinical practice with individuals and families. Mezzo-level social work practice includes practice with larger groups including organizations, schools, businesses, and communities. Direct practice with small groups is variably described as micro or mezzo-level practice. Macro-level practice involves interventions to address larger societal problems through large-scale advocacy on issues affecting entire communities, states, and nations.

115. **B.** The social worker should first discuss her concerns regarding unethical conduct directly with the social worker. According to the *NASW Code of Ethics*, social workers "discourage, prevent, expose, and correct" the unethical conduct of colleagues. Further, social workers should not participate in, nor condone, any type of fraud or dishonesty. In this case, the social worker should first discuss the issue directly with the supervisor in order to discourage and prevent the falsification of records. If that conversation does not lead to the appropriate resolution of only honest documentation being accepted, the social worker should then take further action through appropriate channels.

116. **A.** In explaining the diagnosis of bipolar disorder to the client, including common symptoms as well as treatment options, the social worker is providing psychoeducation. Psychoeducation,

as the name suggests, is a combination of psychotherapeutic and educational interventions that seeks to support a client's treatment or recovery through providing information to assist a client in understanding their symptoms and mental health needs. Psychoeducation is typically provided in combination with other treatment approaches.

117. **C.** The social worker should first acknowledge the client's experience and feelings. This scenario appears to take place at a possible first meeting, as there is no mention of an ongoing social worker - client relationship. Therefore, the social worker's early responses should be focused on the engagement phase of the helping process. Acknowledging the client's experiences and feelings is the most direct response to the client's stated complaints and serves to validate the client and develop rapport. The other possible responses might at some point be appropriate, but they are not what the social worker should do first.

118. **B.** Alprazolam, also known by the brand name Xanax, is a benzodiazepine (tranquilizer) medication that is used to treat anxiety and panic disorders. Other conditions are treated using different categories of prescription medications. Schizophrenia is typically treated using antipsychotic medications such as haloperidol (Haldol), risperidone (Risperdal or Perseris), Zyprexa (olanzapine), and others. Depressive disorders are typically treated with antidepressant medications, such as the selective serotonin reuptake inhibitors Prozac (fluoxetine) and Zoloft (sertraline), the serotonin and norepinephrine reuptake inhibitors Cymbalta (duloxetine), Effexor (venlafaxine), and others. Attention-deficit/hyperactivity disorder (ADHD) is typically treated with stimulant medications such as Adderall (amphetamine and dextroamphetamine), Ritalin (methylphenidate), and Vyvanse (lisdexamfetamine dimesylate).

119. **C.** The most likely explanation for this child's behavior is normal separation anxiety. Separation anxiety is a normal developmental phenomenon for infants and toddlers. In many children, signs of separation anxiety peak around 3 years of age and then diminish. When infants and toddlers experience more intense worry or dread regarding actual or potential separation, or when children or adults experience significant separation anxiety beyond the toddler years, they may meet criteria for separation anxiety disorder.

120. **B.** The student is most likely using the defense mechanism of displacement. Displacement is a psychological defense mechanism, or ego defense, in which a person redirects emotions or impulses from one object, or person, to another. In this example, the student is angry with his father, who has been yelling at him and threatening him physically. He likely does not have the safety, nor the skills, to express his anger toward his father directly. Through displacement, he instead expresses the anger through bullying others.

121. **C.** The client's most likely DSM-5 diagnosis is borderline personality disorder. Borderline personality disorder, also known as BPD, a mental health disorder that involves instability in

mood, behavior, and overall functioning. Because of the person's unstable emotions, they often act impulsively and have chaotic interpersonal relationships. Individuals with borderline personality disorder often describe feelings of emptiness and a fear of abandonment. Borderline personality disorder is treated with evidence-based practices including dialectical behavior therapy (DBT) and mentalization-based treatment (MBT).

122. **C.** In very limited circumstances, it is acceptable for social workers to accept goods or services as payment for services rendered. However, the *NASW Code of Ethics* also states that bartering should be avoided (in most cases). Social workers should explore and participate in bartering when it is an accepted practice among professionals in the local community, when it is necessary in order for service provision, when it is negotiated without any coercion, and when initiated by the client and with the client's informed consent. The *Code of Ethics* further states that, when accepting goods or services as payment, it is the responsibility of the social worker to be able to demonstrate that this arrangement will not be harmful to the client nor detrimental to the social work relationship.

123. **C.** Lack of interest in social activities is not a symptom of antisocial personality disorder. Popular usage of the term "antisocial" generally describes individuals or behaviors that are *asocial*. Asociality describes the avoidance of social interactions and a lack of interest in others. Antisocial personality disorder, on the other hand, involves a pattern of behavior that demonstrates a disregard for, and violation of, the rights and feelings of others. Individuals with antisocial personality disorder show a pattern of engagement in criminal behavior, a lack of remorse for their actions, ongoing irritability and aggression, and other related symptoms.

124. **D.** The client's most likely DSM-5 diagnosis is borderline personality disorder. Borderline personality disorder, also known as BPD, a mental health disorder that involves instability in mood, behavior, and overall functioning. Because of the person's unstable emotions, they often act impulsively and have chaotic interpersonal relationships. Individuals with borderline personality disorder may exhibit idealizing as well as devaluing in their perception of others. This shift between idealizing and devaluing is referred to as splitting. Borderline personality disorder is treated with evidence-based practices including dialectical behavior therapy (DBT) and mentalization-based treatment (MBT).

125. **C.** The social worker should refer this student for psychological testing. Since the social worker believes that the student may have a learning disability, the next step in the assessment process is to determine whether or not this is the case, and to obtain more information regarding the nature of the possible learning disability. Social workers typically do not conduct psychometric testing, and should be careful to practice only within the scope of their license. Therefore, referral for testing is the next step before developing any plan or beginning any treatment.

126. **D.** The husband's most likely DSM-5 diagnosis is narcissistic personality disorder. Individuals with narcissistic personality disorder display exaggerated feelings of self-importance even as they also experience low self-esteem. Narcissistic personality disorder is characterized by a sense of entitlement, a need for constant admiration, and the exaggeration of achievements and abilities. Individuals with narcissistic personality disorder have significant interpersonal difficulties and have difficulty regulating their emotions and behavior. Treatment options for narcissistic personality disorder include mentalization based treatment, schema focused psychotherapy, and transference-focused psychotherapy.

127. **B.** The client's most likely DSM-5 diagnosis is antisocial personality disorder. Antisocial personality disorder involves a pattern of behavior that demonstrates a disregard for, and violation of, the rights and feelings of others. Individuals with antisocial personality disorder show a pattern of engagement in criminal behavior, a lack of remorse for their actions, ongoing irritability and aggression, and other related symptoms. For a diagnosis of antisocial personality disorder, which is only made for individuals at least 18 years of age, there must be evidence that the person previously had conduct disorder, typically with symptoms beginning before the age of 15. This client's reported behavior around the age of 14 meets this criterion.

128. **B.** Dialectical behavior therapy (DBT) is the treatment for borderline personality disorder that has the strongest empirical evidence of its effectiveness. Dialectical behavior therapy is a comprehensive treatment that includes individual therapy sessions, group skills training, in-the-moment telephone coaching, and the therapist's participation in a consultation team. It is a type of cognitive behavioral therapy that treats the emotional dysregulation associated with borderline personality disorder and other mental health and substance use problems.

129. **B.** The next step the social worker should take is to assess the family's eligibility for food and housing assistance. According to Maslow's hierarchy of needs, physiological needs (which include food and shelter) are the first level of human needs. The family's physiological needs must be met before they can address higher level needs.

130. **A.** The primary reason for documentation in a client's chart in a hospital setting is for continuity of care. Accurate, complete, and timely documentation allows for collaboration among the various professionals involved in a client's care. This allows for optimal decision making based on the most recent and complete information about a client's course of treatment, and prevents the duplication of services. While documentation does serve a risk management function, and is necessary in order to meet legal requirements, these are not its primary purpose.

131. **B.** The social worker should speak with the student about this behavior and have them go home for the remainder of the day. As a supervisor, the social worker is responsible for the student's ethical conduct and cannot allow them to remain in the clinic after drinking during work hours.

In this case, the social worker should discuss the issue directly with the supervisee in an effort to prevent this behavior from continuing. If it does continue, however, the social worker should then also take further action through appropriate channels.

132. **C.** The social worker should first acknowledge the complaints and thank the staff members for sharing their experiences. Validation and listening communicate respect and are essential to creating a healthy workplace culture. After doing this, however, it is important for the social worker to gather more details about the nature of the complaints, and then to follow through with meaningful action to address the issues that have been raised.

133. **D.** This finding supports the measurement tool's inter-rater reliability. Reliability is a research term that describes the consistency of responses over time. Among the multiple types of reliability is inter-rater reliability. Inter-rater reliability describes the degree of agreement between multiple individuals who observe responses or phenomena and assign ratings or codes to their observations.

134. **B.** Speaking with a client's family members and obtaining additional information regarding a client's functioning is an example of collateral contact. Collateral contact refers to communication with outside sources of information, such as family members as well as other treatment providers, which can be an important aspect of client assessment. Of course, it is important to obtain the client's consent before sharing any information with collateral contacts. Using collateral information as part of the assessment is consistent with systems theory and the person-in-environment perspective. Collateral contacts can be a resource as the social worker and client collaborate on assessment and treatment.

135. **C.** The social worker should involve First Nations people in service planning and provision, seek out cultural competency training to learn best practices for working with First Nations people, as well as acknowledge the social worker's White privilege. However, the social worker should not position themself as a cultural expert – no matter how much they learn about the community in which they work. Rather, the social worker should adopt a stance of cultural humility and respect the knowledge and expertise of their clients based on their lived experience.

136. **B.** Based on the transtheoretical model, the client is most likely in the contemplation stage. During the contemplation stage, the client has acknowledged a desire to change without a specific commitment. The client may see the need to change a behavior but may still be working through the pros and cons. In this stage, the social worker can help the client articulate their reasons why they desire to change, and help the client begin to make a plan.

137. **C.** A psychoeducation group for injured workers that focuses on pain management and improving quality of life is an example of tertiary prevention. Tertiary prevention refers to an

intervention provided after individuals have an illness or injury. Tertiary prevention strategies help people to manage long-term problems while preventing further worsening and maximizing the person's quality of life. Often, tertiary prevention requires an individualized approach in order to help clients manage complex and long-term conditions, though group approaches can also be effective.

138. **A.** The social worker should first educate the parents about obsessive compulsive disorder and the cognitive behavioral therapy process. It is common for clients and families to desire and expect progress within the first few sessions. In most models of psychotherapy, significant progress does not typically occur this quickly. The parents in this case may not have yet been informed about this, or may need reassurance regarding this issue. If, after providing this psychoeducation, the parents still wish for the child to meet with a different social worker, this request should be honored.

139. **A.** Standard deviation is a measure of the extent of deviation for a group of data points from the group's average value. If a data set has a low standard deviation, this means that its values are close to the mean of that data set. On the other hand, in a data set with a high standard deviation, the values tend to be more dispersed from the mean. Range refers to the difference between the lowest and highest values in the data set. Central tendency refers to the typical value in the center of a data set, and can be measured as the mean, median, or mode.

140. **B.** With regard to accepting payment for services, social workers should take into account clients' ability to pay; should explain their policies regarding payment, including how non-payment will be handled; and should accurately bill for services provided. In general, social workers should not accept payment in the form of goods or services. While bartering is not entirely prohibited by the *NASW Code of Ethics*, the *Code of Ethics* does state that social workers should avoid doing so, and that bartering may be acceptable only in very limited circumstances.

141. **C.** This question asks specifically about the application of systems theory to an understanding of this student's likely experience. Systems theory, in social work, refers to the idea that individuals should be understood within the context of their social environment. Systems are collections of related parts that function together. A change in one part of a system affects the entire system. A person is themself a biological and psychological system, and each person is also a part of family, organization, community, national, and global systems. Problems in multiple systems may all play a role contributing to the client's presenting problems, and resources across multiple systems can all contribute to the client's strengths and resilience.

142. **B.** The social worker's approach is based on a harm reduction model. Harm reduction refers to public health policies and practices that focus on engaging directly with people who use substances, with an emphasis on preventing overdose and disease transmission, and to improve the

physical, mental, and social health of people who use substances. In contrast to abstinence-based approaches, harm reduction seeks to lessen the negative physical and social consequences for people who use substances rather than requiring that people stop using.

143. **A.** This study can be best categorized as exploratory. Exploratory studies seek to create a background for further study. Exploratory research is typically unstructured, collecting qualitative data from small samples. Explanatory research, on the other hand, creates relationships between variables to identify patterns, trends, and possible causal relationships. Descriptive research is more structured than exploratory research and seeks to collect specific data based on research questions and hypotheses.

144. **C.** The social worker should first validate the client's feelings. The client has described feeling angry and hurt, and this should be acknowledged. Assisting the client in filing a formal complaint may be relevant later on, if the client wishes, but should not be the first social worker's first response. Asking about the client's gender identity or earlier experiences would not be relevant in this situation.

145. **B.** The client's most likely diagnosis is autism spectrum disorder, which is a neurodevelopmental disorder affecting how people communicate, interact, learn, and behave. People with autism spectrum disorder experience difficulties in the areas of social communication and interaction, as well as restricted and repetitive behaviors. Intellectual developmental disorder is also a neurodevelopmental disorder, but involves difficulties in general intellectual functioning such as learning, thinking, reasoning, and judgment. Specific learning disorders are characterized by difficulty in reading, writing, and/or mathematics.

146. **B.** The social worker should next acknowledge the client's lack of choice regarding treatment. When working with court-mandated and other involuntary clients, social workers should pay attention to the challenges of engagement as well as their dual roles and responsibilities in relation to the client and the court. The social worker's best response, and effort at building rapport in this instance, is to validate the client's experience. At this point there are not yet any treatment goals to refer back to. The social worker cannot assure any client of absolute confidentiality, and in court mandated treatment there are particular limits to confidentiality as the social worker must report compliance or noncompliance, and possibly more detailed information, to the court. Further, the social worker should not describe services as voluntary, since this would not reflect the reality of the client's experience.

147. **B.** The social worker should first explore the client's feelings regarding the diagnosis. While there is significant stigma about all mental health and substance use disorders, there is particular stigma around the diagnosis of borderline personality disorder as it is sometimes used as a pejorative label. While the diagnosis can in many cases be helpful and even at times validating, as it can explain

a person's experiences, the diagnosis can also be experienced as hurtful or invalidating. Exploring the client's feelings is the best first step in this case, and may be followed by providing psychoeducation. Self-disclosure by the therapist may or may not be helpful, but is not appropriate as a first response in this moment.

148. **C.** Exploring the ways in which the client has unique talents and opportunities is most reflective of a strengths perspective. While the other answer choices may or may not be appropriate depending on other clinical factors, this question asks specifically about the strengths perspective. The strengths perspective focuses on clients' abilities, talents, and resources, using clients' strengths and assets to assist in addressing problems and achieving goals. The strengths perspective represents an alternative to a pathology-oriented approach.

149. **D.** This client's experience likely reflects internalization of the homophobic statements that he has heard in his family. Internalization refers to the unconscious assimilation of attitudes or behavior that then become integrated into one's identity or sense of self. Internalized homophobia, more specifically, is the taking in of biases, prejudices, and hatred toward gay people from the society and turning this homophobia back on oneself. This can lead to self-hatred and shame for LGBTQ people.

150. **D.** According to Freud's theory of psychosexual development, this student is currently in the genital stage. The genital stage begins and puberty and continues throughout adult life. During this stage, the start of puberty brings an active libido and a reawakening of sexual attraction. Freud theorized the source of pleasure as heterosexual relationships and sexual intercourse. A fixation at this stage, Freud believed, could lead to "perversions" that prevent healthy sexual relationships. With the ego and superego fully developed, individuals are believed to manage their desires and keep them within social standards.

151. **B.** According to the life course perspective, the term *cohort* refers to segments of a population that are born in the same time period. An understanding of birth cohorts in the context of historical time allows the taking into account of generational and age-based differences that impact individuals' biopsychosocial development, opportunities in life, and the impact of societal expectations.

152. **B.** The father's behavior is most reflective of attunement. Emotional attunement in parenting involves a responsiveness to the child's emotional and physical needs. It involves considering the likely thoughts and emotions of the child, and using language and behaviors based on that awareness. Attunement supports healthy attachment and emotional development in the child.

153. **B.** The hereditary disease is most likely autosomal recessive. In human genetics, autosomal refers to the carrying of genetic material on a non-sex chromosome; that is, any chromosome other

than the X and Y chromosomes. Recessive conditions are those that may be carried but not expressed when inherited by only one parent, as there would need to be genes for the disease inherited from both parents in order for the person to experience that disease. In this case, as these individuals are carriers for the disease but have not had any symptoms, it appears to be a recessive condition. It cannot be a Y-linked condition as the wife is a carrier but, as a cisgender woman, does not have a Y chromosome. Cisgender refers to individuals whose gender identity aligns with their birth sex.

154. **C.** This question asks specifically about a narrative therapy approach, and so the social worker is most likely to focus on the family's stories about the events they experience. Narrative therapy helps clients to understand and deconstruct the stories they tell themselves and the stories that shape their lives, and then to challenge and reconstruct those stories to shape new realities for themselves. This is believed to help clients to see alternatives and ways through impasses at which they have been stuck. In this case, the social worker focuses on the family's stories in order to help the family client system develop new ways of seeing their interactions.

155. **B.** The social worker must report abuse to the child protective services agency right away. Social workers are mandated reporters of suspected child abuse or neglect, as well as abuse or neglect of elderly people and other vulnerable adults. As a mandated reporter, the social worker is responsible for making a report anytime there is suspected abuse or neglect of a child. This does not require the social worker to investigate further, although that may at times also be appropriate depending on the setting and situational factors. While consulting with a supervisor may also at times be appropriate or necessary for the social worker's assessment or intervention process, making the report of child abuse comes first and is not contingent on any supervisory guidance.

156. **B.** The social worker should first thank the client for sharing this with the social worker. Acknowledging the client's disclosure about her gender identity the pronouns that she uses is the most appropriate first response. There is no indication that the client requires a referral to a specialized LGBTQ+ agency at this time, though that may be helpful at some point. Asking the client about her plans for physical transition, as well, might be appropriate at some point but would not be a helpful first response.

157. **B.** The social worker's interventions are likely to focus on the Eriksonian psychosocial developmental stage of industry vs. inferiority. This stage takes place for children between approximately 6 and 12 years of age. During this stage, school-aged children are tasked with learning how to act and create in their environment. Mastery of this stage creates the capacity for children to see themselves as productive and able to contribute. However, if children are not adequately recognized for their efforts, they may instead develop a sense of inadequacy and inferiority.

158. **B.** The client's experience of fatigue and amotivation is the client's presenting problem. In this case, the reason for referral and the presenting problem are somewhat different. The client was

referred to the college counseling center by his academic advisor based on what had been observed by others: the client was sleeping all day and missing most of his classes. However, upon meeting with the intake social worker, the client described the problem differently. The client stated that he has been tired all the time and does not feel motivated to do anything. This is the presenting problem.

159. **C.** The social worker should first conduct a biopsychosocial assessment. The client appears to be in crisis, and the first stage of crisis intervention is a biopsychosocial assessment, which should include a suicide risk assessment. While helping the client with coping strategies may be needed, intervention should not come before the assessment phase has been completed. Similarly, the client's possible need for shelter services would be ascertained as part of the assessment, and so a referral should not be the first step.

160. **D.** Based on the client's symptoms, the client most likely has panic disorder. Alprazolam is a benzodiazepine and is used to treat anxiety and panic disorders. Risperidone is an antipsychotic medication and is used to treat schizophrenia. Haloperidol is also an antipsychotic medication used to treat schizophrenia. Amitriptyline is a tricyclic antidepressant used to treat major depressive disorder and some pain syndromes.

161. **A.** The intervention most likely to help this client obtain needed health care services is to connect the client with health care clinics that offer free or low-cost services. While conducting a community needs assessment may yield helpful information about the larger need for health care services among undocumented residents in the community, it would not address this specific client's short-term needs. Similarly, while connecting the client with an immigration attorney could potentially be helpful, this also would not address the immediate need for healthcare.

162. **B.** The purpose of follow-up after termination is to ensure that clients have followed up on any referral, and to see if any new needs have arisen. After termination, it is a good practice to follow-up with clients in order to ascertain whether or not the client has connected with any referrals that were given, as well as to determine whether recurring problems or new problems have arisen. Follow-up is also useful in finding out the extent to which the interventions provided were effective, and the extent to which those benefits have lasted after some time.

163. **B.** In client-centered therapy, the factors of congruence, unconditional positive regard, and accurate empathic understanding are all needed in the client-therapist relationship. Congruence refers to the therapist's genuineness and openness in communication with clients. In other words, the therapist's internal and external experiences are one and the same (i.e., congruent), and there is no facade. Unconditional positive regard involves a nondirective, nonjudgmental therapist showing complete support and acceptance of the client. Accurate empathic understanding, according to

Rogers, is more than a reflection of feelings. It involves an in-the-moment presence and attunement to the client's feelings and experiences.

164. **C.** In response to the client, the social worker should first acknowledge the client's feelings. The social worker should also explore the client's experience during the time that the social worker was away, as the client is describing significant emotional content regarding this time. In response to the client's desire to provide feedback to the agency, the social worker should inform the client of agency processes for receiving feedback. Reminding the client that he was informed in advance about the social worker's vacation would not be helpful, especially as the complaint is not related to not having been told in advance.

165. **B.** In exploring which tasks are overwhelming to the client, and helping the client to divide these issues into more manageable units, the social worker is using the technique of partializing. Partializing is a technique in which the social worker helps a client to break down problems or goals into less overwhelming, more manageable parts. Partializing supports a client in seeing some results more quickly as they can achieve smaller goals one at a time. Interpreting, or interpretation, refers to a therapeutic technique in which the social worker goes beyond what the client has said in the moment and instead goes deeper, helping the client to see new meanings and identity connections between past and present experiences. Reflecting, or reflection, is a technique in which the social worker paraphrases or restates the client's words in order to communicate understanding.

166. **C.** In preparing a case presentation, the social worker is likely to include the assessment, diagnosis, and treatment plan. Process recordings are a social work supervision tool in which the social worker, or more commonly the social work student, learns and refines interviewing and intervention skills by examining the dynamics of a social worker and client interaction in detail. These would not be needed in the multidisciplinary team. Instead, a case presentation would use a summary of the assessment, diagnosis, and treatment plan rather than the high level of moment-to moment detail contained in a process recording.

167. **C.** Wellbutrin is an antidepressant belonging to the category of norepinephrine and dopamine reuptake inhibitors (NDRIs). NDRIs are less likely than selective serotonin reuptake inhibitors (SSRIs) to cause sexual side effects. Both Prozac and Zoloft are SSRIs, and clients who take these medications often experience sexual side effects such as lower libido, difficulty reaching orgasm, and difficulty obtaining or maintaining an erection.

168. **A.** Ego strength is a psychoanalytic concept refers to the ability of the ego to mediate between the impulses of the id, which is based on the pleasure principle, and the superego, which is a self-critical conscience, along with the demands of the external reality. Indicators of high ego strength include flexibility, compassion toward others, and tolerance of disappointment.

Egocentrism, which refers to a focus on oneself without attention to the feelings, needs, and desires of others, would not be an indicator of high ego strength.

169. **A.** The experience of the social worker is most likely a result of White privilege. The concept of White privilege describes the advantages that White people experience based on their race in the context of racial inequality and injustice. This is the most likely explanation for the disparate treatment experienced by the client and by the social worker. Gender stereotypes describe societal expectations regarding how members of a certain gender behave or should behave. Gender stereotypes do not appear to be relevant in this situation. Inclusion refers to practices and policies of providing equal access to resources and opportunities, including to marginalized groups. The client's experience in this scenario appears to be the opposite of inclusive.

170. **A.** The client's most likely DSM-5 diagnosis is somatic symptom disorder. Somatic symptom disorder is characterized by a person's high level of focus on physical symptoms, and emotional distress that the person experiences related to their preoccupation with their symptoms. Fibromyalgia involves widespread pain, which this client does not describe as there is only a mention of stomach pain. There is no evidence of schizophrenia based on this case example. Factitious disorder involves pretending to be sick, or causing oneself to become sick or injured. There is no evidence of this, either, based on the case description.

Jeremy Schwartz, LCSW is a social work author and test prep coach with extensive clinical practice and teaching experience. He is the author of *Pass the LMSW Exam: A Practice Test for the ASWB Master's Level Social Work Licensing Examination*, also available from Seeley Street Press. A 2011 recipient of the NYU President's Service Award, he has served in teaching roles at New York University and at the Icahn School of Medicine at Mount Sinai, and has provided tutoring to social workers preparing for the Bachelor's, Master's, and Clinical level ASWB® examinations. A skilled clinician, he has treated hundreds of patients both in private practice and at The Mount Sinai Hospital, where he served on the Professionalism Committee in the Department of Social Work Services.

Reach out to Jeremy at jeremy.d.schwartz@gmail.com to arrange private tutoring.

Get additional practice with original, never-before-published test questions in *Pass the LMSW Exam: A Practice Test for the ASWB Master's Level Social Work Licensing Examination* by Jeremy Schwartz (Seeley Street Press, 2022).

Pass the LMSW Exam is available in paperback at Amazon.com, Barnes & Noble, or your local bookstore. To support your local bookstore while shopping online, you can purchase a copy through Bookshop.org or IndieBound.org. You can also ask your public or academic library to purchase a copy.

An e-book version is available for Kindle, Nook, and Kobo e-readers, and can be requested through your local library's Overdrive site.

Pass the LMSW Exam: A Practice Test for the ASWB Master's Level Social Work Licensing Examination

by Jeremy Schwartz, LCSW

Seeley Street Press, 2022

ISBN (paperback): 979-8986557007

ISBN (e-book): 979-8986557014

CPSIA information can be obtained
at www.ICGtesting.com
Printed in the USA
BVHW011201221122
652279BV00040B/512

9 798986 557045